"Will remind you of a day when football was still a wild wonderful game—more like mock-war than chess, more like life."

—*Book Bag Reviews* (Rockland, Maine)

"Pont takes us inside the college football world as only an insider could. The book captures the personalities of the coaches it covers and makes us yearn for yesteryear."   —*Soundings*

"What distinguishes this mix of memoir and sports history is the author's affection for her subjects and her ability to relate the personal interaction between the legendary coaches and their families. . . . Pont effectively combines savvy football analysis with perceptive reflections on the bonds that held this family of coaches together. A treat for anyone who cares about the history of college football."   —*Booklist*

"Sally Pont has woven well the history of all these coaches and she has wonderfully captured the personality of each."

—Ara Parseghian

"A wonderfully warm and intimate story of the 'Miami Loop,' the cradle of coaches that the brilliant Sid Gillman and his wonderful wife Esther unknowingly founded. Sally's father, being a member of that coaching loop, gave her personal reflections of these fine coaches and their families."

—Paul Dietzel

Fields
of
Honor

Also by Sally Pont

Finding Their Stride:
A Team of Young Runners
and Their Season of Triumph

Fields
of
Honor

---

*The Golden Age of
College Football
and the Men
Who Created It*

Sally Pont

A HARVEST BOOK
HARCOURT, INC.
San Diego   New York   London

www.HarcourtBooks.com

Library of Congress Cataloging-in-Publication Data
Pont, Sally.
Fields of honor: the golden age of college football and
the men who created it/by Sally Pont.—1st ed.
p. cm.
ISBN 0-15-100607-5
ISBN 0-15-602704-6 (pbk.)
1. Football coaches—United States—Biography.
2. Football—Coaching—United States—History.
3. College sports—United States—History. I. Title.
GV939.A1 P63 2001
796.332'63'0973—dc21   2001024364

Text set in Century Old Style
Designed by Kaelin Chappell

Printed in the United States of America
First Harvest edition 2002

A C E G I K J H F D B

To my first heroes,
my favorite Yale football players:
Dick Jauron,
Bill Crowley,
Jeff Roher,
and Joe Pont

Contents

15
Daughters 161

16
Heart 171

17
One Scrappy Kid 181

18
The Press 191

Afterword: My Dad 201

Chronology 209

Memorable Games of the Golden Age 213

About the Coaches 215

Index 219

Acknowledgments

In the throes of writing this book, I entitled it, in my own mind, *How Much Do I Love My Dad?* I believe *Fields of Honor* is, essentially, a love story—for those I love, about those I love. That my wonderful editor Jane Isay indulges me in the writing of such love stories is just one indication she is a great lover herself—of all the love stories there are to be told. I am so grateful to her for having allowed me the opportunity to pursue this labor of love. She knows that a labor of love is, somehow, not laborious at all. That's her secret to being a great editor.

Out of love for my father, for football, and for their own families, the coaches depicted in these pages flung open their doors and entertained me with great hospitality and a treasure trove of stories. John and Sandy Pont, Bo Schembechler and his son Shemy, Steve Hayes, Sid and Esther Gillman, Ara

Parseghian, Bill and Ellie Mallory, Nick and Marilyn Mourouzis, Carm Cozza, Paul and Anne Dietzel, and Don Nehlen were overwhelmingly kind to me. Though I was initially inclined to tremble in the presence of such greatness, they made me feel, invariably, like I was a long-lost daughter come home.

My dear friends Lisa Roney, Amy Lehman, and Max Lehman housed and fed me along my journey, lending me their ears and their thoughts with the unquestioning generosity that is love.

Out of their love for football, two young men, Rahul Rohatgi and Travis Neff, assisted me in research; their discoveries and observations were rubies and pearls. Others, Steve Bloom, Lauren Cook, Lynne Klasko, Andy Terker, and Eamon Murphy, offered their services to me in a variety of fashions, and added a bit of fun to the entire process. Though the isolation of writing is generally unavoidable, these wonderful assistants gave my soul moments of respite.

I am deeply indebted, also, to Jennifer Aziz, Gayle Feallock, and Rachel Myers at Harcourt for their attentiveness and commitment to this project.

Always, my ever patient husband Steve was inspiration and solace. He piloted these pages to their final destination, reading through revision after revision. I am glad he, too, loves football, and I thank God he loves me.

Preface: Love

Shemy Schembechler loves his father, Bo. Shemy was conceived by Bo and his wife Millie in the first days of 1969, just as Bo was deciding to leave his position as head coach at Miami of Ohio. He had been there six years, accumulating a 40–17–3 record, but he chose to part with that success to assume the helm of the troubled program at the University of Michigan. Late in January, he left Millie, newly pregnant with their son, to begin work. On the drive from Oxford, Ohio, to Ann Arbor, Bo's car broke down—an ominous foreshadowing of things to come. But the omen proved false; in mid-September that first season opened favorably for Bo, for Michigan, and for Shemy, with substantial wins over Vanderbilt and Washington.

Shemy was born the week after the victory over Washington, just before the game with Missouri. The 40–17 loss hurt.

Nevertheless, Bo won all but one of the following regular season games, capped off in November by an emotionally charged upset of Woody Hayes's then unbeaten Ohio State team, the game that took Michigan to the Rose Bowl and launched Bo's career.

That was a victory for Shemy as much as anybody. Thereafter, he became the golden child of Ann Arbor. A wide-faced scamp with an "I-know-what-you're-thinkin'" smirk, he grew up under a sunny blaze of maize and blue. Bo let him run wild through practices, equipment rooms, and locker rooms. Shemy hounded players, more often than not winding up facedown in a laundry bin full of sweaty towels.

When he was still quite young, Shemy took his first road trip with the team, to the University of Minnesota, where he spent time before the game playing with Minnesota coach Joe Salem's two sons, both Shemy's age. As the crowds of spectators filed into the stadium and filled their seats, the boys went to their fathers' respective benches and watched from opposite sides of the field as a Michigan team dismantled Minnesota. It was the kind of rout Michigan and Shemy were used to.

But by the end of the game, Shemy heard something he wasn't at all used to. The cursing from the crowd of outraged Minnesota fans was palpable, surrounding him. It was all directed at Bo. In Ann Arbor, Shemy didn't hear words like that. In Minnesota, they pelted him like hail. He couldn't help but burst into tears.

After the game, Bo knelt down to comfort his son. "People are gonna say things about me. You just can't listen to 'em."

Shemy learned not to listen, but shutting it all out couldn't have been easy. Winning and losing evoke complex emotional responses from coach as well as from son. Whenever Shemy and his mother found themselves watching football games on television, they did so in separate rooms because the tension of each drove the other crazy.

To the family of a football coach, no monster, alien, or ghost is scarier than a loss. Down in Columbus, Steve Hayes, Woody's son, was often possessed in his youth by the terrifying thought that every Ohio State loss meant his family would have to move. Woody's winning percentage at Ohio State was .761, Bo's at Michigan was .796, totally irrelevant statistics to quote at the end of a botched game. Memory of past victory means nothing in the face of a loss. Steve, Millie, and Shemy's reaction was more than a desire for father and husband to succeed; it was personal; it defined them. Winning was heaven; losing was a nihilist abyss.

The comments of the fans and the media are not that which really hurts, but they don't help. The Sunday morning sports page can, for any coach's kid, ruin a perfectly good bowl of corn-flakes. Though Bo had so much success, Shemy heard over the years a fair balance of praise and damnation. Like the president of the United States (and Bo's career at Michigan spanned those of Johnson, Nixon, Ford, Carter, Reagan, and Bush), the head coach of such a high-power program is subject to perpetual scrutiny. Although Bo consciously avoided the press as much as he could, often remaining sequestered in Michigan Stadium long after games were over, everyone still found plenty to say about him. He was a public figure, public domain.

My father, Richard Pont, as offensive backfield coach at Yale University for twenty-eight years, was also public property. When I peruse my memory of his career, only the moments of glory come to mind—Kenny Hill's hundred-yard kickoff return at Cornell in 1978; a seventy-seven yard touchdown resulting from Pat O'Brien's lateral to John Spagnola, who proceeded to hit Brian Krystyniak with a beautiful pass to secure a 35–28 victory over Harvard in 1979. While it was all going on, though, the losses evoked feelings that eclipsed all others.

Few children get to watch their father do what he does: no surgeon operates with his kids peering into the cavity of a human body; no Wall Street buyer takes his kid onto the floor of the stock exchange every day. Even fewer watch their fathers in so public a forum as a football stadium. The experience is both exhilarating and exhausting. Sometimes it's too painful to bear. Shemy's peers had their own methods of accepting or avoiding loss. When Nick Mourouzis was an assistant under John Pont at Northwestern University in the mid-seventies—a time when winning was so rare it was greeted with as much incredulity as jubilance—his son Ted and one of his friends would position themselves, one on the top row of seats in the stadium, one on the ground outside. They would pass a football, up and down, until the game was over.

Even though Ted wasn't watching, he was still aware of the game and of his father. He regarded them through two eyes: one doubt, the other faith. For any child, it's hard to control which will triumph over the other. In *To Kill a Mockingbird,* Jem and Scout watch their father defend in court a victim of racism and then lose. They never doubt him, but they pay for their faith. Even so, they would never want their father to be other than he was.

Like Jem and Scout, Shemy felt every emotion on his father's sidelines, but he always kept his faith. He doesn't love his father because it's easy. In fact, his affection and loyalty are the result of the tests he withstood at the hands of publicity, of fickle public sentiment, of football. When Shemy heard the jeers, he saw that in the eye of the Charybdis stood his father, always fighting to stand erect. Looking back at that, Shemy knows he was the luckiest kid in the world to be the son of such a man.

When I first met Bo Schembechler, just a year ago, he offered me a chocolate chip cookie. I am a grown woman and he is an ever growing legend, but he held out a brown paper bag, cookies scuffing against its waxy interior, though it was ten o'clock in the morning, I was late, he wanted to golf, phones were ringing, and a tape recorder was running. Bo's a big guy, a former tackle who played, coached, and preached a hard-nosed style of football, but the bag in his hand, as he extended it, somehow suited him. In shorts and a Michigan blue-and-maize–striped polo, body trimmed of a great weight by the shrug and exhale of retirement, he was a father asking me to be his daughter.

I took the cookie.

It's hard to imagine any famous person, let alone a football coach fabled for bluster and toughness, being endearing. At Kentucky, Texas A&M, and Alabama, Bear Bryant stood on a platform to talk to his team and his coaching staff; he did not tolerate interruption or contradiction. At Miami of Ohio, Northwestern, and Notre Dame, Ara Parseghian drilled through flesh and bone to the heart of his players just with the gaze of his eyes. At Ohio State, Woody Hayes sent his coaching staff on a run up the stadium steps because he thought they were out of shape. Up close these men were incessantly demanding; from a distance they were blocks of granite.

I hardly had a chance to nibble on the cookie, conversation escalated so quickly. Bo could rattle off all the numbers; he could relay victories with jubilant precision and defeats with sardonic shrugs. He almost laughed when he mentioned the heart attack that quelled him the day before his first Rose Bowl at the end of his first season at Michigan, a true foreshadowing of his ten trips to the Rose Bowl (more than any other coach) and his eight defeats (more than any other coach). With the same blithe candor, he described his time as assistant coach under Ara Parseghian at Northwestern, helping to successfully turn around a program from an 0–9 record in 1957 to a 6–3 record in 1959; and under his former coach and mentor Woody Hayes at Ohio State.

He tells those stories without thinking, shifting into the present tense at times to reconstruct a play. All the numbers, names of players, intention, and execution are as vivid to him as if he relived them every day, running them over in his mind like prayers. Offensive lineman Dan Dierdorf, receiver Anthony Carter, and quarterback Rick Leach, as their coach recalls them, seem to materialize in the room.

But then, when I asked him specifics about his family, he stopped to think, a little stumped. People generally ask him about football; they don't want to know what Millie used to make him for dinner.

"Millie was a saint," said Bo as a means of deflection. "She raised the kids."

He means Millie took care of the business of eating, brushing teeth, making beds, raking leaves, getting to school, to the dentist, to lessons, recitals, birthday parties, making sure they had tetanus shots, new shoes, decent grades, morals.

In the same way, Sandy Pont took care of business for her husband, John. When he left Miami of Ohio to assume the head coaching position at Yale University in 1963, he and his coaching staff headed for New Haven as soon as possible, leaving their families behind them. At Yale, the men moved into Ray Tompkins House, the athletic offices next to the gymnasium, so they could dive into the task of recruiting. Sandy ran the house in Oxford with the three Pont children, as she always did.

Her oldest, John Jr., had just started school. The sudden exposure to other children meant, that spring, exposure to illness. John Jr. brought home first Asian flu, then mumps, then rheumatic fever, promptly sharing them with his sister Jennifer and his brother Jeff. Sandy nursed them while their father spelunked the East Coast to put together a Yale team that would have a 12–5–1 record in his two years there.

Like Sandy, Millie was always there for her son Shemy, but he seldom let his gaze leave his father. In his coaching, in its daily struggle to maintain discipline, commitment, and passion, Bo did his own kind of fathering, the kind that every football coach offers to his children.

I am Bo Schembechler's daughter just as much as I am my father's. Bo knows that. That's why he gave me a cookie.

And that's why I accepted.

Ara Parseghian used to play a game called "grizzly bear" with his children, Mike, Karan, and Chris. In his grizzly bear persona, he used to hide in a closet with two sliding doors. His children would search for him while he waited, knowing they would eventually arrive at the closet. When they slid open one door, he stepped behind it. When they slid the other, he stepped behind that. This ruse kept up, amid shrieks of laughter, until Ara let himself be seen.

"Is that the *secret, secret* place?" the children wanted to know, because he had led them to believe there was one place he hid, like no other, magical, that defied all inquisitive children except, perhaps, them.

"No, that's not the *secret, secret* place," their father said. They groaned, despairing at the idea of having to go through the exhaustive search for the *secret, secret* place yet again. They wondered if there would be any chance, ever, for one glorious instant, of rushing in on their father as he crouched in the shadows of that exclusive world.

At some point, I suspect, that's what they found when they went to their father's football games. Inside the throng of delirious Notre Dame fans and under the ambivalent gaze of the media's cameras and microphones, even in such a wildly public moment as the end of the infamous 1966 tie with Michigan State, they had private moments with their father.

I imagine the child of a writer, reading his latest book, feels the same uncontrolled sequence of emotions that Shemy Schembechler, Ted Mourouzis, John, Jennifer, and Jeff Pont, Mike, Karan, and Chris Parseghian, and I felt for so many years.

While I was growing up I felt like an exclusive person for exactly nine Saturdays of the year. Not only did I sit in the stands in Yale Bowl among people much larger than me — one Harvard game, Henry Kissinger sat in our row — I traveled to such exotic places as Providence, Rhode Island, and Ithaca, New York.

The games themselves possessed a magic enhanced by my lack of understanding of what was happening on the field. I fantasized about touchdowns, then celebrated them in my consciousness for a long time after.

Sometimes, though, I saw the designs, or at least their obvious points: the lineman, the hole, the tailback sliding through. The safety cutting inside, picking off a pass. The quarterback bouncing in place, buying time for the bomb.

Nevertheless, football was my father's *secret, secret* place, a world I tried to enter but never fully could because I could not find the door.

I used to believe that the entrance to the *secret, secret* place was an actual door, painted blue, on the outside of Yale Bowl, near portal 16. After games, the players and coaches exited through that door to be cheered by fans and kissed by family. I always tried to peek in to see what mysteries were contained within, but the crush of bodies was so thick it blocked my vision.

When my father was home after a game, calming himself before whatever social event he was summoned to attend, he watched the Prudential College Scoreboard. In the early seventies, when I was first waking up to football, I was a small body outside his field of vision. I thought there was a miasma of random games, random teams like Memphis State, Texas A&M, and Brigham Young that played each other in a vast, uncivilized free-for-all, while the teams in the Ivy League conducted themselves like gentlemen and played each other, systematically. That's why the Prudential College Scoreboard saved the Ivy League scores for the end of the program.

My father, though, was looking at a matrix of football based not so much on locale or conference as on nostalgia. On a Saturday in the early seventies, the Colorado score brought to mind Bill Mallory; Paul Dietzel was at South Carolina; Ara Parseghian was announcing his retirement. In my father's mind, he saw each of them, heard their voices, some stories over a beer or two, and recalled old football games they coached, play by play. He saw their best players, too: Heisman winners like Paul Dietzel's LSU hero Billy Cannon, and Parseghian's brilliant creation at quarterback John Huarte. He saw, too, the scrappy kids who made magic occur on the field: Harry Gonso who was like a son to John Pont at Indiana, and Jeff Hostetler, Don Nehlen's quarterback at West Virginia who actually became his son-in-law. The final score of one game could call to mind an epic narrative. In cinematic fashion, a game like the 1969 Ohio State–Michigan matchup, in which Bo Schembechler, in his first season, shut down Woody Hayes's number one–ranked squad, played itself out in my father's mind. I could see the action depicted in his facial expressions. He was viewing the sepia images of the greatest plays, constructed by the greatest minds.

Within this matrix of images was a center: Ohio. My father and his brother John grew up in Canton, where a teammate of Jim Thorpe was a local cop. Their Timken High School team played the powerhouse that was Massillon High, the program

Paul Brown created; Mansfield High, where Paul Dietzel helped deal Massillon its first loss in nearly a decade; and Canton McKinley, Massillon's perennial foe. Canton football was national news and local mythology. When the Pont brothers and their buddies, playing tackle football on a cinder lot, ran a touchdown past the end zone into the adjacent street, they knew traffic would stop.

Ara Parseghian, in Akron, played halfback. In Barberton, Bo Schembechler was at tackle. Carm Cozza, a three-sport star in Parma, outside Cleveland, dreamed of baseball but clung to football. Bill Mallory lived with his coach in Sandusky to finish his high school football career when his family moved away. Parseghian and Pont found Nick Mourouzis in Uhrichsville, just outside Canton, and brought him to play quarterback at Miami of Ohio. Don Nehlen was a helluva quarterback himself at Lincoln High in Canton, though he, like Cozza, felt a penchant for baseball. Woody Hayes hailed from Clifton, Ohio, and, throughout his career, found no reason to leave the state for more than a few days at a time. Though factories fed and clothed these towns, football inspired them.

There are more figures from Ohio, before and after: Cleveland Browns founder Paul Brown, former Army coaches Colonel Earl "Red" Blaik and Jim Young, recently retired coaches Larry Smith of Missouri and Dick Tomey of Arizona. In Ohio, the spirit of football is palpable.

Why Ohio? Hard to say. The average inhabitant of the state is neither tougher nor shrewder than anyone else in the country; the cities are hardly capitals of a financial and media-oriented world. Really, Ohio—except for Kent State, of course—is and always has been a peaceful place. So why Ohio?

No coach I spoke with could tell me, for certain. Some suggested a work ethic born in the factories of the north and central regions, some pointed to Paul Brown. Most shrugged off the question. Though I was born in Steubenville, Ohio, in 1964, I don't know the answer, either. My father took a position at Yale when I was too young to feel the unifying force of Ohio.

Now I'm beginning to see that certain people created football as we know it, but football created Ohio. It is the turf under every child's feet, the backdrop of every romance, and the narrative of every heroic moment. For that reason, Ohio is my father's home.

The *secret, secret* place is Ohio, but not Ohio of any particular space and time. It is the Ohio that gave birth to the greatest generation of football coaches in the late forties, and the Ohio that wept over Woody Hayes's fateful socking of a Clemson player in the 1978 Gator Bowl. Ohio nurtured them and watched them die. This book reveals what I found to be my father's Ohio: from the dawn to the twilight of the great coaches my father drank with, learned from, and loved. This is my blue door. Come on in.

PART I

Dawn

1

Who's Your Daddy?

The first name in the family tree of Ohio football is Paul Brown, with his Massillon High School machine of the 1930s, a program he had so finely tuned that against them no team for nearly a decade could hold their own. In half a century, Paul Brown replicated the system he created at Massillon in exponentially larger forms, first with Ohio State, then the Great Lakes teams he generated at a World War II naval training station north of Chicago, on to the Cleveland Browns, and finally the Cincinnati Bengals.

The first brain in Ohio football is Sid Gillman. Though many a specific innovation in football was a brainchild of Sid, what he gave to the game was a new way of thinking. While head coach at Miami of Ohio from 1944 to 1947, he single-mindedly turned football into an intellectual game, a chessboard with athletes as the moving pieces. That those pieces were both tough and agile was certainly a boon, but the power of bodies—in Gillman's football scheme—was second to that of the mind.

Though he was from Minneapolis, for over twenty years he found Ohio to be fertile ground for his explorations and innovations. He moved through the state as if following points on a football compass. First, he played at Ohio State, coached there, then at Denison, Miami of Ohio, and finally the University of Cincinnati, where in six years he lost only thirteen games. Though the level of competition and quantity of exposure of each school varied greatly, setting in all cases mattered only in proportion to its ability to house his choreography.

In 1940, the vehicle for well-choreographed plays crystallized in the T formation, an outdated design resurrected and kicked up by George Halas of the Chicago Bears with the help of the brilliant mind from the University of Chicago, Clark Shaughnessy. The new model for the T centralized the quarterback, allowing for a variety of ball exchanges behind the line in even more varieties of direction. In addition, because the ball was kept behind the line of scrimmage for a controllable amount of time, the T formation offered the offense a new weapon with which to attack. The formation demanded taut prescription of each player, but also allowed for surprise.

Paul Brown brought the T formation to Ohio State a few seasons later. Sid Gillman didn't jump on the T formation bandwagon till his 1946 season as head coach of Miami of Ohio. For both, inspiration to apply a de rigueur offense germinated with Francis Schmidt, Brown's predecessor at Ohio State under whom Gillman acted as an assistant. That Schmidt came from Texas Christian was apparent in his phraseology but not in his loyalty. After his first Ohio State team defeated the long invincible Michigan, he drawled, "And as for Michigan...well, shucks, I guess you've all discovered they put their pants on one leg at a time." Really, team loyalty was arbitrary...he was devoted solely to *X*s and *O*s. Using the single wing, double wing, and I formations, he had the capacity to execute three hundred plays with his Ohio State teams.

As the game of football evolved in the United States from its first formal game in 1869, between Rutgers and the College of New Jersey (later known as Princeton), so did the concept of the play. In 1892, a chess player named Lorin F. Deland crafted a play for Harvard's team he hoped would shut down Yale, the dominant force in national football for a decade. Though personality often overshadowed precision in the early years of football, the notion of the play as a set of chess pieces in motion remained.

But the rationale behind plays was still in the process of evolving. At times, they were a means of protection, like the V-trick used by Princeton in 1884, in which the ball carrier was kept snug inside a V-shaped mass of his teammates. Or they were aggressive, such as the V-trick innovation, or "Flying Wedge," proposed in 1892 by Deland, in which the V followed a kicker in a running assault. Plays such as the forward pass devised by Gus Dorais and Knute Rockne at Notre Dame were practiced beforehand to perfection. But the idea of a multipurpose offense that could maintain an integral structure but still change in a myriad of ways did not solidify till the T formation.

Through his use of the various formations, Schmidt's brain controlled the body of his team. For that reason, it is no surprise that Schmidt's pupil, Gillman, did not adopt the T formation till a few years after its debut. Gillman, too, wanted his brain on the field, but localized. With the T formation, he transplanted his brain into a single player. That receptive player simply didn't come along at Miami of Ohio until 1946. When he did, Gillman's new offense was a springboard to his future, and the future of football.

Though he played and coached, Gillman could drop back and assume the role of spectator, always critiquing, always searching for perfection. After his mentor Schmidt left Ohio State and Sid took an assistant position at Denison, Sid needed to find someone or something else to teach him. So he studied his past to answer the puzzles of formation and execution, and to do so, he used films.

For the honeymoon with his new bride Esther, he purchased excellent tickets for the college all-star game in Chicago, which they watched despite a deluge of rain. The day after, in a pawnshop, Gillman spent fifteen of the newlyweds' last twenty-five dollars on a projector he intended to use to analyze films of his players in action.

In his hometown of Minneapolis, his father owned a movie house. Purchasing his own projector to study film, a method unknown in football prior to Gillman, seemed natural. Originally, Esther protested they couldn't spare the money, but once her husband made the purchase, she always hung the white sheet on the wall of their home, onto which a myriad of films were projected, and sat down beside him to watch.

Sid graded film with a scale of points: one for execution, more for taking the play further; negative one for failure to execute, more negative points depending on loss of yardage.

With the detachment of film, Sid's coaching became objective: affirm what was right; correct what was wrong. But it also acknowledged potential for extremes in failure and success. For the players, this led to a moral imperative: if I do what Coach says is right, we'll win. A play frozen on a frame of film could be analyzed, critiqued, praised, and, most importantly, duplicated. Through the study of film, Gillman defined a tidy reality, one that could be replicated perfectly, over and over again.

When he arrived at Miami of Ohio as an assistant to Stu Holcomb, Gillman was still involved in the learning process, and he was having a heckuva good time with it. His notorious, often intimidating intensity was underscored by the pleasure he took in resolving the problems of formation and execution.

In 1944 he replaced Holcomb as head coach at Miami—a fortuitous time. He benefited from the arrival of guys on the GI bill participating in Miami's V-12 program. They were experienced, smart, strong, and used to executing plans. Among them were halfback Ara Parseghian, who came to Miami after honing his skills on Paul Brown's Great Lakes team, and center Paul Dietzel, who left behind a scholarship at Duke to enlist in the Army Air Force, then followed a circuitous route that led to the V-12 program and his high school sweetheart, Ann, at Miami. In 1946 a feisty eighteen-year-old quarterback named Mel Olix joined their ranks.

From among these three Sid selected his first satellite brain.

The logical choice, in light of the T formation, was Mel Olix. But one of the beauties of the T formation is its versatility. The centralized quarterback acts as a locus for a variety of plays, both on the ground and in the air. As a result, a range of personnel on a team are responsible, in an alternating fashion, for moving the ball down the field. In addition, the swift center-to-quarterback connection, unseen in earlier formations such as the single wing, double wing, and box formation, allowed the backfield more time to unravel a play. The team's trio of powerhouses offered a perfect balance for the T formation's geometry: Mel Olix wasn't afraid to handle the ball; Ara Parseghian wasn't afraid to carry the ball; Paul Dietzel wasn't afraid to snap.

Sid drew plays and graded film till the wee hours of the morning.

Between 1946 and 1947, this same lineup saw only three losses and one tie. The losses, all in 1946, were frustratingly close: 13–7 to Purdue, 20–17 to Miami of Florida, and 13–7 against Cincinnati.

Miami had a chance to tie Miami of Florida with a field goal. Sid, though, went for the win, and tried to move the ball on fourth down. They were stopped just a few inches too short.

Ara Parseghian claims responsibility for the loss to Cincinnati. On the final drive of the game, while he was playing defensive halfback, he had mistimed his route and let a Cincinnati pass through, for a touchdown.

Film showed Gillman one thing above all: timing is everything. A pass doesn't have to be pretty if it's timed right. A halfback doesn't need to be big to break through tackles if his timing is right.

Time is a formidable foe, and, unlike a body, it can never be injured.

Timing was among the top priorities in Gillman's training regimen. He counted every step his players took as if they were musical notes, knowing a pass or a tackle would be worthwhile only if it came at just the right time.

Dietzel liked to center the ball with one hand. His coach at Duke ordered him to use two. Gillman wasn't quite so quick to correct. He studied the film first. He learned just how confident Dietzel was with the ball; his snap made Olix's job that much easier. Moreover, Dietzel was a big enough guy to hold the line firm.

And what he realized was that the T formation is much more than a vehicle for the quarterback; it is a systematized way to manage time. Specifically, it allows for the control of the quantity of time the ball remains behind the line of scrimmage. Gillman discerned that Dietzel, more than any of the others, was the time manager.

Dietzel illustrated this role best in the 1947 game against Bradley, in Peoria. Miami had a 26–13 halftime lead, but two botched passes in the second half gave Bradley a 27–26 lead. With less than two minutes remaining, Miami was third and twelve deep in its own territory. Olix delivered a prayer of a pass that was caught on the Bradley thirty-five and brought down on the sixteen. Another pass carried the ball to the four. It was fourth down with twenty-five seconds left. There were no time-outs remaining; there was no time for a huddle. After a quick setup, Dietzel hit a key block that allowed Olix to sneak for the victory.

Gillman left Miami after a 13–12 victory in the Sun Bowl over Texas Tech capped off a four-year career in which he experienced only six losses. He was placing himself under the tutelage of Colonel Earl "Red" Blaik at Army. But Ohio still had its own lessons for Gillman, and Gillman turned right back around to be head coach at Miami's nemesis, the University of Cincinnati.

When Gillman arrived there in 1949 with Dietzel as his able-bodied assistant, many of his former Miami players defected to Cincinnati, but not Mel Olix. Olix was a good quarterback, but he was not the real royalty of Gillman's offense. Paul Dietzel was the prince of time. In other words, he was Sid's son.

Sid had four children, Lyle, Bobby, Terry, and Tom, and a wife named Esther who drained spaghetti in screens removed from her window to feed hungry football teams. They understood that Sid was busy. He stayed in his office deep into the night grading film. He sent out for burgers around midnight. He expected his assistants to stay. They couldn't resist. They loved arguing over what was good, what was good enough, and what was ideal in the increasingly precise game of football.

Really, it was Paul Dietzel's accuracy that guaranteed the success of Gillman's offense. And, on future teams, though Gillman's brain sometimes appeared to be in his quarterbacks, his success was in the responsiveness of other players, at other positions, in their ability to slow—even stop—time.

I imagine Sid in his office at night a mad scientist, poring over film, his assistants in such a frenzy of excitement over the discoveries they were making that they couldn't stop thinking about football.

The play, that abstract narrative suggesting motion, conflict, and resolution, defines football.

Gillman's children were all born in Ohio—Lyle and Bobby while he was at Denison, Terry and Tom in Cincinnati. After he left there to assume the head coaching position of the Los Angeles Rams in 1955, his closest brush at a real return to the sweetness of Ohio football was his 1987 stint as a consultant with the struggling University of Pittsburgh team, forty-five minutes from the Ohio border. Nevertheless, the offspring of his mind continued to play chess in Ohio.

A dynasty, by its definition, is a family affair, a line of power passed from father to son. It implies that gifts are genetic—that a son is as successful as his father because they are the same person, born at different times.

Paul Dietzel thinks of Sid as his father. Ara Parseghian has been Dietzel's brother. Brothers John Pont and Richard Pont lived in Parseghian's basement in Oxford, Ohio, when they first took jobs in coaching, John as Ara's assistant, Rich as a Miami graduate assistant at Sycamore High School in Cincinnati. When Rich coached Steubenville Catholic's team against the best from Ohio, Pennsylvania, and West Virginia, he mimicked Dietzel's defensive concept: the "Chinese Bandits."

And so on, exponentially. College coaches of a generation trace different lines back to Gillman, all hatch-marked by lessons, arguments, and couches to sleep on. That's family.

2

The Relationship Between
Mind and Heart

"The most deceptive course in football is straight at the goalposts," Woody Hayes once mused. "When the Germans went through the Argonne, it wasn't an eighteen sweep, it was a ten trap."

Hayes thought a passing game was a newfangled atrocity, a gamble at best. He believed a fullback up the middle would work time and time again. So when Hayes became head coach of Miami of Ohio in 1949, replacing George Blackburn, defector to Cincinnati after leading Miami for just a single season, Hayes's brain seemed Sid Gillman's antithesis. He was emotion as opposed to reason; he was bombastic, in-your-face, unrelenting. Above all, he was dead set against a flashy, risky style of play. He compressed Sid Gillman's T so that it was a dense mass, literally pushing the ball forward. He returned

the team to a simpler format—focused on block and tackle—
from the gut rather than the mind, and he worked the hell out
of them to get them there.

The Miami players—among them John Pont, Carm Cozza,
and Bo Schembechler—wondered just who this guy was.

He was, as they would find out, just another guy. At that
point, Hayes's football résumé was nothing flashy. It consisted
of four years of high school coaching, only one of them as
head, and three years at the helm of Denison's low-profile
program in which he had played as an undergraduate, intending to pursue studies in law.

But he was a natural leader. He experienced officers' training school and action at sea during World War II. In the Palau
Islands invasion, Hayes was on a PC 1251; then he was transferred to the destroyer escort *Rinehart*. He boarded each ship
as an executive officer. On both occasions, over time, he was
given command. His naval experience broadened his innate
capacity for leadership. It gave him a deeper language with
which to lead, to coach, to speak to his players, many of
whom, because of the GI bill, knew that language, too. He
could rally a disparate group of men. As a coach, he would
often use wartime metaphors to motivate his football players,
groups as eclectic as any he found in the Navy. World War II
had signaled to him—as it had to others involved in the war—
that race and socioeconomic background were irrelevant to
performance.

On the football field he was more than an average guy. He

was omnipresent, even haunting. He chewed out athletes. He would make threats like "No back is worth two fumbles." Bo Schembechler reports that he and his teammates lived in fear of making a mistake. Once during a game, a running back fumbled because, as he reported to his coach, he was hit from behind. Hayes promptly retorted that the player fumbled because he didn't have both hands on the ball. After that incident, a Miami running back wouldn't be caught dead without both hands on the ball. Coach's anger was always at the forefront of their minds.

Though Hayes was a yeller, he didn't opt for volume to make up for lack of content. He knew what he was saying. He said it loud because he was sure he was right. He viewed himself as a student of football, approaching it the way he did history as an undergraduate at Denison and a graduate student at Ohio State. In actuality, under the bluff and bluster, he was just as intellectual as Gillman.

Nor did he yell to draw attention to himself. He was never self-impressed or self-promoting. His leaps into leadership positions were the result of impatience with incompetence rather than ego. He just wanted to make things right for other people.

No, Hayes was no dictator. In fact, he was so egalitarian that he always forgot his own prominence in thinking of others. He was oblivious to how loud and scary he was. He simply realized that he had the resources to elevate and edify his athletes and chose to use them as often as possible.

This egalitarian sensibility manifested itself in a strange di-
chotomy: he wasn't interested in stars on the field; no one got
extra attention or special privileges. Off the field he would
mortgage his home to help any athlete in trouble.

Above all, Hayes believed in education and saw football as
merely a permutation of all a university had to offer. Though
his father had been a teacher and had gone to college, many
of the players he coached—Pont and Cozza, for example—
were the first in their families to have the opportunity. And
Hayes was happy they had the chance, maybe happier than
the players themselves. He believed in it so loudly that everyone around him couldn't help but listen. Even when they
wished he'd keep it down, they all knew he was right.

Because many of Miami's best players had defected to
Cincinnati to play for their old coach Sid Gillman, Hayes's first
season concluded with a record of 5–4. The next season he
set out to right that situation.

Hayes wanted victory for the players. He felt they'd been
cheated. He was angry about losing players to Gillman, even
though the fact that Blackburn went along with them to work
for his old boss got Hayes the Miami job. He was annoyed
that he had lost to Cincinnati in 1949. All around, he wanted to
put Gillman in his place.

Throughout the fall of 1950, a season with only one loss,
Hayes elevated Gillman's castoffs into one of Miami's great
teams. So thorough was Hayes's transformation of these play-

ers, six members of that team—Carm Cozza, John Pont, and Bo Schembechler, of course, as well as Jim Root, who received the Small College Coach-of-the-Year Award in 1968 while at New Hampshire, John McVay, who was at the University of Dayton before moving on to the New York Giants, and Doc Urich, who coached at Northern Illinois—went on to become college head coaches. In other words, they became educators of the Hayes mold, going on to impart values he had originally taught them.

For this group, one game mattered above all else, against Cincinnati. The day of the game, an ominous blizzard howled through Ohio, carrying more than revenge.

No one in Ohio would dream of canceling a football game, especially this one. Their hearts were in it too deeply. In Cincinnati, Miami ran head on toward its nemesis. Their hearts tunneled the way through the snow.

The heroes of the game, which became known as the Snow Bowl, were seeing through Hayes's eyes. One was an unlikely figure, halfback John Pont. He had been turned away from Miami by Gillman a few years before because of his size, but had slipped in during the Blackburn window. The other, at fullback, was Jim "Boxcar" Bailey. The two of them drove their team to a 28–0 trouncing. They did it by the Hayes Method: ball low to the ground, no foolish passing, no risks, just well-executed football. It was all heart and grit.

It wasn't Woody's brain on the field. It was the players as

their best selves. Hayes had exorcised the ghost of Gillman—
his team was his own.

Up in Columbus, on that very same day, Ohio State took on
their own arch rival, Michigan, in the throes of the storm.
Ohio State, at that time the best team in the Big Ten, one of
the best teams, in fact, Ohio State had ever put together, lost
to Michigan by a score of 9–3.

Ohio State players reportedly (and no doubt the rest of the
state) had "tears frozen on their faces." Head coach Wes Fesler
was buried in a barrage of criticism. That game proved to be
his last at Ohio State; he submitted his letter of resignation.

Immediately, there was a groundswell of support, from pe-
titions to newspaper pieces to votes in the state legislature,
for Paul Brown's return to his former job at Ohio State, which
he maintained from 1940 to 1946. And then Don Faurot, head
coach and athletic director at Missouri, was actually offered
the position. But nature prevailed. Brown expressed no interest; Faurot turned the offer down. The snowstorm that
swept through Ohio lost Wes Fesler his job, and got Woody
Hayes his.

Many years later, Woody waxed nostalgic about all the
people he had to thank for providing his life with the richness
it possessed. First was John Pont, star of that Snow Bowl
team. And second was Bo Schembechler, who chose to follow
Hayes's teachings.

But Hayes had thanked them many times over throughout

the years, not with words but with actions. He facilitated their careers. Schembechler eventually joined his staff at Ohio State for a time, as did a player Pont coached: Bill Mallory. That was Hayes's idea of a relationship: from your end, you never stop giving.

In his relationships, Hayes didn't need the upper hand, though sometimes his comportment suggested otherwise. His son Steve tells a story about watching his father during a characteristic fit of anger, flinging plates around the kitchen. Woody's wife, Anne, picked up a whole stack of plates and smashed them all to the floor. Silence descended on the kitchen. Woody knew when he was outdone.

Woody's heart ruled his mind, but his heart could also pacify his mind.

Ohio State, at the time, was known as the grave of coaches. Even the greatest years were scarred with frustration, and losing to Michigan in the final game of the season was every coach's greatest fear. It happened in 1926, when All-American fullback Marty Karow could not prevent the heartbreaking 17–16 finish. In 1935, Francis Schmidt's nearly undefeated team lost hold of a 13–0 lead at the beginning of the fourth quarter against Notre Dame, losing 18–13. Ohio State had some great seasons, most notably in 1919, when triple threat player Chick Harley was unstoppable, and in 1934, Schmidt's first season as head coach. But consistent success seemed to take root everywhere but Columbus. The national eye, in the early part of the century, gazed north, south, east, and west, and most painfully at Ohio State's rivals, at these coaches: Fielding "Hurry Up" Yost at Michigan, Amos Alonzo Stagg at the University of Chicago, Robert Zuppke at Illinois, John Heisman at Georgia Tech. Then there were players like Notre Dame's Four Horsemen in 1924—Don Miller, Elmer Layden, Jim Crowley, and Harry Stuhldreher—and like Red Grange, who played at Illinois in the late thirties, the same era in which Sammy Baugh brought the passing game to new heights at Texas Christian.

Names from Ohio State, at least while they were at Ohio State, never achieved such mythic status.

Paul Brown was a hero, but not because of his coaching at Ohio State; the few years of Ohio State victories were distinguished by a few key people who did not have the backdrop for flash and pizzazz. The dearth of heroes kept Ohio State in the Big Ten doghouse.

But Hayes wasn't interested in the whole idea of heroes. His philosophy was: win when you have talent; lose when you don't. So he got the job.

Ohio has never been the same since.

There is a price for egalitarianism. Everyone has to work equally hard. Hayes was known for his sixteen-hour days. His assistant coaches knew Hayes's habit all too well.

Former Miami quarterback Mel Olix became an orthopedist who practiced in Columbus. Hayes's assistants appealed to his professional insights and succeeded in eliciting Olix's medical opinion that work on Saturday nights was bad for the coach's health. Hayes honored the prescription for exactly one season. Then he forbade his coaches to return to Olix again.

They didn't need to. The collective effort of coaches and players, the sense of shared suffering and joy not unlike that which fellow soldiers feel, kept them going and gave Ohio State the formula for success it had been missing for half a century.

To invest in a single personality is a risky venture. When the board of Ohio State hired Hayes, they didn't know so much about his personality as they did about his style of coaching. And so his personality could coexist with the thorough intensity and the egalitarian quality of his teams. Without the elevation of individuals, the members of the team were closer together, as if they were touching. The mind and the heart don't connect with a pass. The heart stays tight in the body.

3

Knowledge Worth Knowing

After a single year of coaching experience, over the freshmen of Miami, Ara Parseghian was the improbable and therefore perfect successor to Woody Hayes as Miami's head coach.

Why question it? First of all, he was a brainchild of Sid Gillman. Then, his undefeated freshman team gave him a standing ovation at the team dinner. But calls were made to those who knew Parseghian, the crucial one to Paul Brown. Brown had been Parseghian's coach on the Great Lakes Naval Training Station team during World War II, and again with the Cleveland Browns after Parseghian moved on from Miami a year before his graduation. Brown's voice, in Ohio, was the voice of a god.

"Ara doesn't know what he doesn't know," Brown pronounced.

God spoke, and the Miami athletic board only offered Parseghian a position in which he would be coach in name only, but in actuality the workhorse under the authority of John Brickels, who had been assistant under Hayes and was also head basketball coach.

Parseghian said, emphatically, no. He wanted the position, but he needed to *know* he was coach. He knew that a coach could be neither a patsy nor a figurehead.

Someone must have been impressed by his conviction, because Parseghian became head coach in every sense, ushering in a new style of coaching for Miami. Maybe Parseghian didn't know what he didn't know, but he sure knew people. He knew they wanted to believe in themselves and what they did.

Originally, coaching at Miami was not where he saw himself. He left college to realize his dream of becoming a professional football player with the Cleveland Browns. A hip injury his first season prevented Parseghian completing a second, but the desire to play lingered. Forever feeling the sting of his own initial struggle and frustration, he personalized his players' feelings about failure and success, seeing in them himself as he was that year with the Browns. Upon identifying that aspect of his athletes that was so like himself, he was able to inform his men, accurately, who they were. These acts of definition shaped his teams and allowed for the rapid-paced success of his early career.

His empathy was quickly displayed in his first season as head coach at Miami. At 212 pounds, and with a hundred-yard dash time of 9.6, Jim "Boxcar" Bailey, a key figure on Woody Hayes's Snow Bowl team, had the bulk and power to incite in a coach fantasies of touchdowns. The size of players, since the first ink-etching days of the game, had been a topic of interest. The smallness of early Yale players Walter Camp and Amos Alonzo Stagg and the girth of Pudge Heffelfinger assured them not of loss or victory, but simply of notoriety. Athleticism, it seemed, could be measured as much by passion as by height and weight. Bailey was different: his size could win games. But another obstacle stood in his path: he was African American.

Bailey, with Parseghian's team, traveled to Kansas to take on Wichita State. When the Miami team arrived at their hotel, the residents and manager had already heard about Bailey. And they didn't want him in the hotel. He was turned away.

Parseghian did not accept that. He let his athletic director, John Brickels, know that either the team stayed at the hotel together or they didn't stay in Kansas at all. Finally the hotel acquiesced; Bailey spent the night with his team.

Bailey was a player Parseghian defined as well as respected. After Bailey's outstanding 1950 season at fullback under coach Hayes, Parseghian chose to play him at end when necessary. Parseghian's judgment was astute; Bailey was as resourceful in that role as he was in the backfield. That ability to accurately assess and implement a player's talents would serve Parseghian in a number of crucial circumstances.

He immediately made the team his own. His first season he went 7–3, and his second 8–1.

That he "got it" with his athletes was the result of his willingness to listen to his players' stories. He knew about personal, family-related troubles. Some players were married; some were uncertain about their abilities. Parseghian was a surrogate father who could be fair and just. He never asked his players for more than they could give—just 100 percent, that was all. And he knew what 100 percent meant for each athlete.

He was always involved in someone's story because he had such a rich one of his own. His father, an Armenian in Turkey, was the only child in his family chosen to be formally educated. He was sent to Smyrna. When the Armenians were persecuted there, he fled for Greece. He was driven to Marseilles, then to Paris, and found his way to the freedom of Akron, Ohio. He sent for a woman, a seamstress, he had met and fallen in love with in France. He became a banker. He and his wife raised their children in Ohio.

Parseghian's father traversed an indirect route to success. So did his son.

Parseghian didn't know what he didn't know, but he knew who he was, and he knew who his players were.

At Miami he began work on his methods of communicating signals. He kept the decision making on the sidelines, with the coaches, and established an encoded system to call plays to the quarterback. Despite the hundreds of plays in the team's repertoire, he worked with his staff and quarterback to commit them to memory. The code changed to throw off opposing teams. Sometimes, a symbol was as innocent seeming as a coach's stance on the sideline.

He also experimented while at Miami on team communication during the game. Long before other college teams used numbers for the quarterback to call a play at the line, Parseghian did it. After all, he had been coached by Sid Gillman: like his mentor, he wanted action on the field to be wisely timed. He used methods of communication to accomplish this.

Parseghian shaped his team into a successful one. In 1955—his fifth season—they went undefeated, and Parseghian's name was in the national press. Because of Ohio connections—former Miami coach Stu Holcomb was athletic director at Northwestern at that time—Parseghian swiftly moved on to Northwestern, a team that had won no games during the 1955 season.

Though Parseghian had been a head coach only five years, he was able to make the change to higher-profile football because he embraced the dynamism of change. He found it to be good for programs, for individuals...for himself.

World War II marked a change in attitudes toward many things, as Woody Hayes had discovered. Parseghian found himself supporting the changing attitude toward marriage. Immediately following the war, men and women were much more anxious to put thoughts of marriage before career, getting married in their early twenties, even their teens. Parseghian himself was married at the age of twenty-six, during his year of coaching Miami's freshmen, to Katie, whom he had met at Miami. Two years later, he offered his own house as honeymoon residence to his senior captain, Tom Pagna, who had just married his high school sweetheart. It was a gift given out of characteristic empathy, but Pagna was so moved by it, and by so many other countless gestures, that he became Parseghian's most loyal assistant at Northwestern and Notre Dame; in fact, player became son to coach.

Bo Schembechler believes that Parseghian proved his greatness at Northwestern, 1956–1963, where he dismantled a lemon of a team and reassembled it in his first three years. In his second season there, he had no wins, but returned the next season with a new crop of players, finishing the year with a 5–4 record, including wins over Michigan and Ohio State.

Of Schembechler's assessment, Parseghian commented, "Of course Bo would say that. He was on that coaching staff."

But that's Parseghian shucking off much-deserved praise. He has a policy to deflect praise and to accept criticism. A win is the result of great players, staff, fans. A loss is all his own.

By that measurement, his second season at Northwestern was a heavy burden, "traumatic," as he once described it. After the 4–4–1 season of 1956, he realized that two obstacles stood in the way of increased success: the philosophical distance between some coaches and players, and the literal distance between coaches and recruiters. As far as Parseghian was concerned, coaches should lead, coaches should recruit. He asked certain players and all recruiters to leave. In essence, he dismantled the program, stripping away the deadweight of uncommitted players and middlemen recruiters. The remains survived the disaster of an 0–9 record.

The following season revealed the success of Parseghian's personally conducted, meticulous recruiting. The 1958 squad won their opener against Washington State, setting the tone for the season. Big wins over Michigan and Ohio State assured Parseghian of his position at Northwestern.

In 1959 the team maintained the ranking of number two in the country for several weeks; in 1962 they finished the season 7–2, the best record they'd had since 1948.

But Parseghian had only so much he could work with. Because Northwestern was a private university, costs were substantially higher than any other Big Ten school. Moreover, Northwestern limited the number of scholarships to twenty-five. The team lacked a breadth of talent and seemed to lose its spunk by late in the season.

Parseghian coached by means of intuition, focusing on the present or the future, as needed. Intuition told him to get out of Evanston. It told him, too, to continue his ascent to the upper echelons of football programs. When he heard of an opening at Notre Dame, he made a phone call.

Notre Dame was out of the Miami loop. Miami was provincial; Notre Dame was national, even international, in its visibility. Miami was a pastiche of ethnicities and religious backgrounds; Notre Dame was Catholic.

Again, Parseghian didn't know what he didn't know. So the

Armenian Protestant with the gumption to make a phone call found himself at Notre Dame. There, he acquired a team that had, since 1956, been in a slump—five straight seasons without a winning record—out of which three different coaches could not lift them. In 1963 they won only twice. Parseghian's Northwestern squad had overpowered them in four straight matchups.

Because of the weight of history at Notre Dame, elevating the program would require all the intuition that Parseghian possessed. In his first months at Notre Dame, he trusted it completely.

During spring practices, in front of thousands of fans, he told his new players that they did not "own their positions." After challenging them with surprise after surprise, he made some radical changes. He rearranged the personnel, changing the positions of nearly every player on the team. He redefined established players; among them were the four veteran running backs known as the "Elephant Backfield." He shifted Paul Costa, 240 pounds, to defensive end; fullback Pete Duranko, 235 pounds, became a defensive tackle; Jim Snowden, 250 pounds, assumed the more appropriate role of offensive tackle. Parseghian told them who they really were.

But he also took advantage of the opportunity to mold players who bore resemblance to no one else. He chose John Huarte as his quarterback for his newness. Though Huarte was to be a senior, he had played third string the previous season. Parseghian chose to shape him into a rarefied personification of the ideals of Ara Parseghian: he charged himself and his staff with the ultimate goal of giving Huarte confidence.

The coup of the outset of his career in South Bend might have been his power over Notre Dame fans. They were captivated by him. One night in January, before Parseghian had done little more than hold meetings, he and his assistants were distracted from their work by a disturbance outside. Through the window, they saw hundreds of students waving torches, booming "Ara! Ara! Ara!" to the frosty sky.

That summer, Parseghian threw out the old football helmets that were adorned with shamrocks, and changed the color of the uniform jerseys from green to gold and blue. His stamp on the team was complete.

But he had to win. In the fall, he charged his team: "To be great, to achieve, you must earn the right."

They seemed to have imbibed his words already, anticipating them before he even spoke them, the achievement was so swift and intense. In one of the most remarkable turnabouts in football history, Notre Dame defeated nine teams in succession, averaging thirty points a game while holding their opponents to an average of six. After everyone's incredulity wore off, Notre Dame was picked as the nation's top team. John Huarte's confidence grew all season, as he created a deadly combination with end Jack Snow.

Huarte earned the Heisman Trophy honors before his team's final game against Southern Cal, boosting his confidence still further. During the first half of the game, he and

Snow connected with ease. At the end of the second quarter, they went into the locker room with a 17–0 lead.

Southern Cal scored quickly in the second half. Then Notre Dame responded with a drive to the Southern Cal one-yard line, and the fullback blew in.

But the touchdown was called back. And with that ruling, the confidence of Parseghian's team crumbled. They lost 20–17.

"We wanted to bring back the national championship," he said to the crowd in the Old Fieldhouse.

"*You did!*" the crowd shouted back.

Parseghian seemed to fear that he had lost his connection to the Notre Dame fans. But, as his great friend Tom Pagna wrote, "If he talks to you, you're his."

When the time came to accompany Huarte to the Heisman awards ceremony, Parseghian had to rent a tuxedo. He hadn't known he was ever going to need one.

Gillman and Hayes redefined football, making it more cerebral, more lofty. Parseghian did that and more: he redefined himself again and again. Three times he redefined a team, and all along, he jostled and kneaded everyone with whom he had contact. Parseghian didn't know what he didn't know, but he knew what he needed to know: that knowledge doesn't make things happen, people do.

4

Little Brother

The story goes that in 1945 at Miami, coach Sid Gillman took one look at John Pont's 149-pound frame (Pont later admitted that the storytellers exaggerated generously on the detail of his weight) and told him succinctly to go eat a steak and be on his way. Pont's way circled through military service back to Miami. While Gillman was coaching at Cincinnati during the Snow Bowl of 1950, he watched his misjudgment play itself out. No player ever scared him the way Pont did. Even if Pont looked as if he could be stopped, he simply couldn't.

John Pont was the improbable and therefore perfect star of Woody Hayes's 1950 team, as well as Ara Parseghian's team of 1951. More improbable were his records: in each of his three years of playing he was named an All-Mid-American Conference halfback; he scored twenty-seven touchdowns; he gained 2,390 yards in 340 rushing attempts; he returned thirty-three kickoffs for 874 yards. Perhaps most improbable, considering the names of other Miami graduates—from Paul Brown to Ara Parseghian—his number 42 jersey was the first retired.

Lots of improbable things happened in that era. World War II altered many lives, and the GI bill sustained many of those alterations. Like Parseghian, Pont enlisted (after Gillman turned him away from Miami), and, while stationed in San Diego, he learned to play halfback. This route took him, via the GI bill, back to Miami. He knew the GI bill was too good to pass up, so he revisited Miami with a friend of his from home. The friend went home after twenty-four hours, but with Gillman gone, Pont was happy to hunker down in Oxford. That he waited tables three meals a day in a women's dormitory to pay his tuition was no burden to him, as it allowed him to play football in a place he loved. He was only too happy to return there, after a one-year stint in Canadian professional football, as Ara Parseghian's freshmen coach making only $4,000 and living in Parseghian's basement like a son just on the brink of adulthood.

Growing up, Pont had learned the value of hard work and the need for self-sacrifice. In the thirties, his hometown, Canton, Ohio, smelled like rubber, steel, and processed chicken meat, but it was known for its football. Pont went to Timken High School and played football on a team with far less prominence than two other local high schools, Massillon and Canton McKinley. Because Pont's father worked swing shift, he couldn't take time off from the steel mills to see his son play in the games that were traditionally held on Friday nights. A recent immigrant from Spain, he was never given the opportunity to understand the local obsession with football.

Young John Pont was given the opportunity, and he understood completely. He played tackle football on a cinder lot with his friends, running plays straight into the adjacent street, while one of his friends stopped traffic. Traffic stopped. In Canton, everyone understood.

Pont's father fully learned to appreciate football when his son attended Miami. In 1950, he came to Parents' Day at Miami of Ohio. When they announced that he was the father of John Pont, number 42, the roar in the stadium was deafening.

That Pont's father was so long in coming to football might offer an explanation for the fact that Pont always treated teammates and, eventually, his coaching assistants, as younger brothers.

Brothers, to Pont, were those you worked with and for, not competed against. As a result, when John's little brother Richard went to conference foe Bowling Green at the same time John was in school at Miami, it was not a comfortable rivalry for the older brother. He felt no impulse to combat his brother, and did not relish the two victories his team earned. In their second meeting against each other, in Oxford, Richard was playing with a broken collarbone. Of course the older brother couldn't say anything, and no doubt his younger brother wouldn't have appreciated intervention, so John Pont fumed to himself over the insensitivity of the Bowling Green coach.

Pont may have been little, but he was always the big brother.

There were other "brothers." Pont roomed with teammate Carm Cozza, and was best man at his wedding. As soon as Pont landed the head coaching position at Miami, he pulled Cozza from coaching high school ball and playing semipro baseball to join him. In Oxford, they lived down the street from each other. Another assistant, Ernie Plank, lived with his family across the way. All their children played together, and their wives traded recipes. It was an idyllic time of collective living. The coaches would often find time to walk home together for lunch.

There were other brothers from outside the world of football. The best man at Pont's wedding was his best friend from Canton, a fellow Spaniard named Fatty. Though Fatty remained in Canton, on the other side of the state, he still lived in Pont's world. Fatty would bring busloads of folks from the old neighborhood to many a Miami game, carrying with him a healthy store of the Spanish foods Pont loved.

Loyalty was the underscoring quality of this brotherhood. It was a quality that was promoted not just by Pont, but also by the entire Miami community. Pont got a good taste of it at the beginning of his career as head coach.

In 1956, when Ara Parseghian took the head coaching position at Northwestern, he offered to bring his assistants along, leaving Pont, the freshmen coach, behind. All but one member of Parseghian's staff decided to go. Who would succeed Parseghian at Miami was not altogether clear.

Then one day in the football offices, athletic director John Brickels stopped Pont, asking him if he wanted the newly vacated position. When Pont responded affirmatively, Brickels blurted, "Well, why don't you tell somebody?"

A few days later, Brickels picked up Pont in his car. In the passenger seat was the president of the university. As they drove past the fraternity houses on campus, Brickels turned around and asked Pont, "Do you want the job?"

At twenty-seven, Pont became the youngest head coach in the country. Pont told his players to call him either "Coach" or "John." He sensed there would be times when the players would need to feel on equal footing with their coach. Besides, he knew he was going to have to earn his players' respect in more ways than name.

The coaches, among themselves, could be little boys. The Miami coaching staff, during the fall, ate with the players at the training table. Prior to games, steak was the traditional meal. Jay Fry and Ernie Plank would each flank Pont, knowing he wouldn't finish, each ready to spring for the remaining piece of meat. That was the only real competition among these brothers.

Perhaps because of his little brother, Bowling Green became the focus of Miami's most intense rivalry during Pont's coaching years.

Though Pont's first season at Miami's helm would be considered by most to be a success, the frustrations seemed to eclipse the victories. The record was 7–1–1; the two nicks were a 7–6 loss to George Washington in the season opener and a 7–7 tie with new nemesis Bowling Green.

Miami had been leading the game by a 7–0 score when Bowling Green blocked a Miami punt. The result was a touchdown and extra point for Bowling Green, creating the final score of the game. The tie cost Miami the Mid-American Conference championship title, which they had held during the two final years of Parseghian's reign.

The following year, 1957, the more experienced team and coach still found themselves at halftime of the Bowling Green game tied at 7–7. The teams went up and down throughout the third quarter without a score. In the fourth quarter, after a long series of downs, Miami punched the ball in from the one-foot line, but Mack Yoho, the kicker, missed the extra point.

Bowling Green matched Miami's drive down to the ten-yard line. Miami's defense slowed them down, and Bowling Green was held on fourth down at the one-yard line by a much-redeemed Mack Yoho. The resulting 13–7 victory gave Miami the Mid-American Conference championship to which they had grown accustomed.

The next year, Bowling Green staged an attack in the first half that led to a 14–0 lead over Miami. During halftime, Pont spoke to his athletes with such fiery rhetoric that they bounced around the locker room, banging into each other. They took their energy onto the field and won 28–14.

On Friday nights before games, Pont slept well. But on Saturday nights he tossed and turned, second-guessing the decisions he had made in the game that day. Usually his anxiety was unfounded. With all the rivalry focused on Bowling Green, Miami dealt with their high-profile opponents more handily. And big wins like the 1962 10–7 upset of Purdue caught the attention of Yale alumni in Chicago, such as 1937 Yale football legend Clint Frank, who contacted Yale athletic director DeLaney Kiphuth about Pont when Jordan Olivar stepped down.

After Pont spent three seasons as freshmen coach and seven as head, Miami had molded itself comfortably into his home. But he brought many of his brothers with him when he departed. Most of Pont's staff traveled to New Haven, leaving behind only Woody Wills and Wayne Gibson, who stayed on at Miami. For the first few months, Pont and his staff lived like a religious brotherhood cloistered in the stone walls of Yale's athletic building.

Yale was a different scene for this son of Ohio, but Pont was not one to be easily intimidated. On the final night of his interviews, he was taken to Mory's, the private Yale restaurant steeped in tradition and lore, by members of the Y Association.

It was their turf, not Pont's. He held his own, though. After a few drinks with him, the Yalies, as Pont described, "let their hair down."

Nevertheless, when Pont had been at Yale just a few weeks, DeLaney Kiphuth informed him that they were going into New York City for lunch, as a group of Yale alums wanted to meet him. Kiputh sped the green coach to Manhattan.

They arrived at a brownstone that had a bronze plaque fastened by the burnished door. Inside was a world completely new to Pont. There were bankers and businessmen discussing the far-reaching arena of finance while Pont could only politely listen.

What's this football coach doing with these people? he thought to himself.

Other aspects of life at Yale also required adjustment. The setting was urban; coaches lived far from each other, in different towns; a qualified football player might not be qualified enough for Yale. But the football—the history, the Yale Bowl with its regular crowds of fifty thousand, the players themselves—took no adjustment time at all.

Even Yale was not removed from the world. Pont's first Harvard game in 1963 was postponed a week because of the assassination of John F. Kennedy. The president, who was a Harvard grad, had been intending to attend the Game in the Yale Bowl. Pont heard the news of the shooting on Friday afternoon during the junior varsity game. Yale postponed the Game to let those from both Harvard and Yale mourn.

Yale won that game. Pont had two strong years at Yale, with records of 6–3 and 6–2–1. As Pont was still in his thirties, it was no surprise that another school looked his way.

The return to Indiana was a return to his roots. Carm Cozza stayed behind, assuming Yale's helm, but Pont returned to his brothers.

To replace his dear friend Cozza, Pont invited a former Miami player, quarterback Nick Mourouzis, to join his Indiana coaching staff. Like Pont's, Mourouzis's parents had immigrated from the old country, Mourouzis's from Greece. Pont's and Mourouzis's feelings of pronounced ethnicity created a bond that underscored so many of Pont's relationships. When he was a kid, his neighborhood football team consisted of Spaniards, Italians, Hungarians, and Syrians. At Miami, he was known as "Spik"; Cozza was "Wop"; Schembechler was "Kraut"; Parseghian was dubbed "Rug Cutter" and "Brahma the Bull." The differences in family background only served to establish a familial connection. Mourouzis quickly became Pont's little brother.

Mourouzis hailed from Uhrichsville, Ohio, just south of Canton. He had been recruited to Miami by Pont in 1955 and ten years later joined in Pont's effort to beef up the Indiana program with some recruits from their colorful portion of the world. While driving through Ohio, Pont and Mourouzis were in a car accident that hospitalized both, but the scare only brought the two men closer together. Their joint effort paid off—among several Ohio boys who signed with Indiana was a quarterback named Harry Gonso from Findlay, Ohio, who had been turned away by Ohio State because he was too small.

So Gonso was another little brother for Pont to add to the family.

Pont inherited a program in need of a little love and affection. In the six seasons prior to Pont's arrival, Indiana finished no better than second to last in the Big Ten. Though it took two seasons for the effects of Pont's recruiting to come to fruition, that third year, 1967, delivered.

In eight games, Indiana went into the last four minutes of the game with a scoreboard hinting at defeat. They won all eight because of Pont's trust in Gonso. Gonso called his own plays, and made some shifty gambles late in games to convert loss into victory. Against Iowa, down 17–14 with fifty-three seconds left in the game, Gonso tricked the Iowa defense with a fourth-down run from field goal formation to set up the winning touchdown, then hit it with a pass to flanker Jade Butcher.

After defeating Illinois, Michigan, Wisconsin, and Michigan State, Indiana was undefeated, ranked fifth in the country with their eyes set on the Rose Bowl. When they faced Minnesota, though, it seemed they were shooting too high. Minnesota was also a Rose Bowl contender, and against them Indiana's gutsy style of play led not to magic but to mismanagement: a fumble, mistimed blocking on a kickoff, a pitchout to no one, and two passes to ineligible receivers—one of which, a touchdown catch, was ruled no good. Minnesota dominated for a 33–7 victory.

But Indiana did not avert its gaze from the prize. Though the team fell in the polls, they met undefeated Purdue—a fourteen-point favorite—in their final game undaunted. The defense shut down Purdue's All-American halfback, Leroy Keyes. In addition, Gonso turned his magic back on. With only six minutes remaining in the game, and a slim 19–14 lead, Gonso was backed against his own end zone. Under that immense pressure he took the type of gamble he was known for: he called his own play. With a pass to Butcher, he dug Indiana out of the hole they were in and secured the 19–14 final score.

With a final record of 9–1, Indiana shared Big Ten honors with Minnesota and Purdue, gaining admission to the Rose Bowl because Indiana had not been to Pasadena as recently as the other two teams had. In fact, Indiana had never been to the Rose Bowl; they had never played a single bowl game.

Moreover, their coach had never before been named Coach of the Year, but shortly after the loss to USC in the Rose Bowl, Pont received that honor. Pont woke up little Bloomington as if it were a child on Christmas morning and gave it a gift. His was an act of brotherly love.

5

Wunderkind

Unlike his teammate Ara Parseghian, Paul Dietzel knew what he didn't know. Sid Gillman must have told him. After graduating from his role at Miami as Sid Gillman's on-field brain, Dietzel let Gillman take him on as apprentice when, in 1948, Gillman made his own pilgrimage to the feet of Army coach Colonel "Red" Blaik, another former Miami coach. Always, Gillman provided his charge with the finest teachers. More than once, Dietzel had to make choices between them, first selecting Gillman over Colonel Blaik in 1949 when Gillman left Army for Cincinnati, then Bear Bryant at Kentucky over Gillman in 1951, and again back to Blaik in 1953. As if these gurus weren't enough, on one occasion, a fellow named Biff Jones stepped up to play that role for Dietzel as well.

In addition, Dietzel began to attend clinics run by another Miami man, Paul Brown, who was at that time with the Cleveland Browns. Then someone stole Brown's playbook and there were no more clinics. But Dietzel learned a great deal about organization from Brown, which he applied when he was an assistant under Colonel Blaik at Army for a second time, in 1953.

Dietzel was a son with many fathers. For what is a father but someone who acknowledges a kindred spirit and tries to guide and promote him?

They all chose Dietzel for his brains and his gumption. During his first staff meeting at Kentucky, Bryant drew a play on the blackboard, narrating the particulars. He turned to his assistants, asking their opinion. "Fine," said one. "Fine," said another. "Fine." Until they got to Dietzel. "Coach," he said, "I'd do something a little different."

Bryant rifled the chalk at him. Writing and talking, Dietzel rerouted the play.

At the end of the meeting, the other assistant coaches crowded around Dietzel.

"Boy," said one. "That was great how you stood up to Bear."

He was gutsy enough to drink all the know-how out of his mentors. Though he learned organization from Brown, discipline from Bryant, control from Blaik, and innovation from Gillman, he was not really much like any of them. He fused all their talents into a kind of creativity that was sometimes over the top and a little nutty. Through all the organization and discipline, Dietzel maintained an attitude of warmth and exhilaration: he regarded everything that happened on a football field as infinitely entertaining, so much so that he could laugh out loud to watch it or even to think about it. The Germans have a word for young men like Dietzel: *Wunderkind.* The term implies not only brilliance but also a childlike sense of delight or wonderment at the results of his own talent.

Dietzel showed early signs of this heightened pleasure when he was defensive line coach for Gillman at Cincinnati. There, he often liked to draw cartoons or to clip headlines or articles out of the newspaper to use as inspiration for his athletes. One day, on the funny pages, in a comic strip called "Terry and the Pirates," a character named Chopstick Joe was talking about Chinese Bandits: "There's one thing about the Chinese Bandits: they're the meanest, most vicious people in the world." So he posted this comic strip, dubbing his six-man line and two linebackers the Chinese Bandits. As this group practiced by themselves, on a cinder field with no lines, without the defensive secondary because those players doubled as the offensive secondary, this label gave the eight-man group a sense of identity that was both colorful and inspiring. And it was just wacky enough to really stick.

At that point, Dietzel must have realized he had sufficiently internalized Gillman's genius. He joined Bear Bryant's staff at Kentucky for two years as offensive line coach. After that important stint he returned to West Point to jump-start his tutelage under Colonel Blaik.

Placed in charge of recruiting, Dietzel kept a set of charts with a graph for each state in the country, listing senators, how many appointments each could make, their principal nominations to West Point, and their three alternates, most of which could be football picks. He'd spend an awful lot of time on the phone with former Colonel Biff Jones, his chief recruiting connection in Washington, D.C., who would go to senators to talk them into letting a football recruit become an alternate.

By 1955, when he was offensive line coach for Colonel Blaik, Dietzel knew his apprenticeship was nearly up. He had learned well. He received a phone call from his friend Charlie McClendon, one of the assistant coaches at Louisiana State University, who reported that the head coaching position was available. "You should try to get this job," said McClendon.

Dietzel protested that he didn't even know where LSU was. Besides, he didn't have any real contacts.

McClendon sighed. "If only you knew Biff Jones."

"Know Biff Jones!" exclaimed Dietzel, and his contact was made.

Biff Jones, it turns out, was far more than a retired colonel with a passing interest in football. He had been head coach at LSU when Huey Long was still alive. During a game in which the team was losing, Long, along with his bodyguards, tried to get into the LSU locker room so he could talk to the team. Jones barred him. When the team went onto the field for the second half, Jones walked up to the president of the university and resigned.

Shortly after, Long swaggered up to the president of the university and demanded that Jones be fired.

"I can't fire him," said the president. "He just quit."

Long, outsmarted by a mere football coach, walked away with a little less swagger.

Jones recognized in Dietzel a younger version of himself. Though he warned Dietzel that politics would always be the most difficult part of the job, Jones knew his protégé could handle it with the aplomb he once used.

Dietzel, at thirty, clean-cut from his time at West Point, was a welcome sight in Baton Rouge. When he was first introduced to about fifteen thousand members of the student body in LSU's agricultural arena during a boxing match, he was greeted with five minutes of applause.

At first, Dietzel delivered. LSU won its opening game in 1955 against Dietzel's old team, Kentucky, 19–6. The town was confettied with reveling. The players and staff were on top of the world. At a party after the game, one of the LSU assistant coaches said to a Kentucky coach, "The trouble is, you guys aren't tough anymore."

The celebrations and the bragging were premature. That first season ended with a record of 3–5–2. The next year, Kentucky beat up LSU, and Dietzel's record was worse than the year before, with three wins and seven losses.

Dietzel started to use his brain: something was wrong with the system. Biff Jones had warned him about politics; he determined to gain control of the political situation that was affecting him at LSU. In this instance, the politics inhibiting Dietzel's performance did not come from within Louisiana but from across the border, over in Texas.

Dietzel became aware that his old boss, Bear Bryant, at that time at Texas A&M, was employing a few illegal methods of recruiting Louisiana players, siphoning away some of the state's finest talent. Bryant was given permission by the president of the Louisiana Gas Company, who was an alumnus of Texas A&M, to use the Louisiana Gas airplane for flying recruits and the families of players to games; a high school player that both Texas A&M and LSU were recruiting turned up with a new car. Dietzel knew Bryant's methods from years before, knew Bryant was as unlike Dietzel's Ohio colleagues as a man could be. So he got Bryant on the phone and threatened to turn him in if he didn't stop doing that sort of thing with Louisiana boys. "You're taking the food off my children's plate," said Dietzel.

Bryant knew Dietzel, too. He knew Dietzel was serious. "Okay, Pablo," Bryant conceded. "We won't."

From that moment, LSU lost no more players to Texas A&M. As a result, Dietzel was able to pick up one of the finest players in LSU history, just down the road from the university in Baton Rouge: Billy Cannon. Even if Cannon had been the only player Dietzel brought to LSU after standing up to Bear Bryant, he would have been enough.

A player such as Cannon—6'1", 210 pounds, able to deadlift five hundred pounds and pluck the ball out of the air at a full sprint—is a welcome addition to any team. Cannon worked with legendary strength coach Alvin Roy to perfect the combination of bulk and speed. Nevertheless, Dietzel's program still lacked the sheer mass of bodies that makes a larger program so successful. At that time, athletes generally played both offense and defense. Also, the substitution rules at that time allowed a player to reenter a game only once per quarter. Because of these two factors, Dietzel's first-string players were exhausted by the end of the game, performing far below their ability. So he devised a system of three eleven-man teams that would go on and off the field en masse; as a result, no single group of players would be overburdened. The first group, which he dubbed the "White" team, were the first-string players, who could easily shift from offense to defense. They would play half a game. The second team, called at first the "Gold" team and later the "Go" team, somewhat skilled but not so athletic, would be coached to play offense, solely. And for the third team, Dietzel resurrected the concept he had devised while working under Sid Gillman at Cincinnati: coached to play defense only, the third-team members became the Chinese Bandits.

Dietzel put the combination of Cannon and the three-team system into motion in 1958. They handily defeated Rice in their first game, but the secret ingredient of the season's success did not emerge until the second game.

In that game LSU went up against Alabama. It was Bear Bryant's first year there. When the stands collapsed early in the first quarter, no one left. This, everyone seemed to feel, would be a game worth standing for.

In the first quarter, Cannon broke loose for a long run, but just before he was knocked out of bounds at the forty-yard line, he let go of the ball. An Alabama player scooped it up and nearly scored, but was stopped by the LSU offensive end at the three-yard line. Dietzel knew Alabama was going to score, and he didn't want the White team to be demoralized, so he put the Chinese Bandits in. The Bandits held Alabama's offense for three downs and made them kick a field goal. LSU won the game 13–3.

Two weeks later, before the Florida game, the proprietor of a local restaurant made up a thousand coolie hats to pass out to students. At the same time, a disc jockey in Memphis contacted Dietzel with a "Chinese Bandit Chant" he had written. The LSU band director quickly worked it into his repertoire.

At the end of the first quarter, Dietzel relieved the White team, substituting with the Bandits. The students pulled out their coolie hats, and the band struck up:

> Chinese Bandits on the way
> Listen to what Confucius say:

On the first play of the drive, Florida ran an off-tackle formation; when the Bandits hit the fullback, the ball popped up in the air. One of the Bandits caught it. Because he only knew defense, he had no idea what to do with the ball, so he downed it. The Bandits charged off the field before the band finished the chant:

> Chinese Bandits gonna chop
> Gonna stop a touchdown, chop chop.

Soon the Chinese Bandits became the stuff of legend, not just to fans, but to members of the team. All the players wanted to be Bandits.

Because of an injury to first-string guard Ed McCreedy, one of the Bandits, Tommy Lott, was moved up to the White team. After the new roster was posted, there was a knock on the door of the coach's dressing room. It was Lott.

"Can I see you, coach?" Lott asked.

"Yeah," said Dietzel. "What is it?"

"I notice my name is up on the White team."

"Yeah, I don't know if Ed can play, and we need someone who can do defense, so you've got to play."

"Well..."

"I moved you up to the *White* team."

"That's okay, coach, but is this permanent?"

"Well, no."

"Good, because I want to play with the Bandits."

Freshmen, who were not eligible to play varsity at that time, approached Dietzel, asking if they could try out for the Bandits.

Dietzel's brilliance in re-creating the Chinese Bandits was part of the reason for the undefeated 1958 season, the winning of a national championship, and the naming of Dietzel as Coach of the Year. But, in the end, his confrontation of Bear Bryant affected his career most profoundly.

This became evident during the 1959 Halloween game against Ole Miss, considered to be one of the best games of the century. The two teams went in ranked second and third in the country, but just before kickoff of the evening game, everyone learned that the number one team in the country had lost during the day. The squads were so evenly matched that one sportswriter made this prophesy: a single, great athlete would tip the balance of the game.

Though LSU fumbled three times in the first half, Ole Miss converted for only one field goal. Ole Miss concentrated its energies on trying to throw off the three-team system by punting the ball more frequently than necessary, thus wearing down LSU's White team.

With the score still 3–0, Ole Miss was punting yet again in the fourth quarter. The ball hit the ground at the fifteen and took a high bounce. Dietzel had a rule about punts: a player should never handle a punted ball inside the ten-yard line. Cannon was standing on the five-yard line. Dietzel, seeing that Cannon was reaching for the bounce, called out, "No, no!" But Cannon didn't hear, and he ran past the Ole Miss bench, eighty-nine yards for a touchdown. With the extra point, the score was 7–3.

After a long drive in which they had to go for it on fourth down more than once, Ole Miss found themselves on the LSU three-yard line, first and goal. Billy Cannon, at linebacker, stopped the ball on the one-yard line. On the next play Cannon knocked fullback Charlie Flowers back to the two-yard line. Then Flowers plunged off tackle, and Cannon thrust him back to the three-yard line. Ole Miss decided to go for it on fourth down. Their third-string quarterback, known to be a runner, came into the huddle. Sure enough, Ole Miss ran a quarterback keep around the end. Cannon tackled him on the three-yard line, securing LSU's victory.

Dietzel still laughs when he recalls that his eight-year-old son Steve, sitting in the stands, turned to his mother during that goal-line stand and said, "Will my Daddy lose his job if we lose this game?"

Dietzel laughs over his Bandits, too, over the luck of his knowing Biff Jones, over his assistant coach trash talking to his counterpart from Kentucky. He even laughs a little bit at Sid Gillman's football monomania. It's easy to laugh, I suppose, when your 1958 team has a record of 11–0 and is named one of the best teams of the century, when the hometown boy single-handedly wins one of the best games of the century, and when that game leads to that hometown boy winning the Heisman Trophy. Above all, it's easy to laugh when you're a wunderkind.

6

Full Circle

When Woody Hayes's son Steve was old enough to learn football, Woody drilled him on the field in Ohio Stadium in the basics and subtleties of playing. In other words, he stood on a tackling sled and Steve pushed it around the field.

One scalding summer day, Woody was called out of town, but he informed his son that one of the assistants would give him his scheduled workout.

In light of the cruel weather, Steve felt mighty relieved. He knew any assistant would last about five minutes in that heat.

To his surprise, practice in the sweltering sun went on and on, through drill after drill, seamlessly, neither longer nor shorter than Hayes would have gone. Straddling the sled, Bo was the living replica of Steve's father.

The assistant, Bo Schembechler, knew how to be Hayes, and wouldn't have dreamed of being anyone else with Hayes's son. In many ways, he and Hayes were mirror images of each other, as true rivals often are.

The journey to that summer day in Ohio Stadium was circular: it began and ended with Hayes not as rival, but as mentor. Even as teacher and pupil, they were already so much alike. They both played tackle. They both believed that academics came first. The girth of both was substantial. They both lived and breathed football all day, every day. They had tempers. Though Schembechler's father was a fireman and Hayes's an educator, each somehow sapped the urgency of one father and the integrity of the other, welding the two qualities together into their aggressive style of coaching.

In 1949 at Miami, when Steve was an infant, young Bo Schembechler sized up new head coach Woody Hayes. He saw not only himself, but also that which he would become: a guy who cared too much.

There were many stops along a circuitous route toward that self-acknowledged destiny, but the pivotal moments involved Schembechler squaring off with some permutation of himself.

The first incident occurred during the Snow Bowl, 1950, the confrontation of Sid Gillman's Cincinnati team with Hayes's Miami athletes. Though Gillman recruited Schembechler in 1947, he only coached against him. When Gillman assumed the head coaching position at Cincinnati, he drew the head coach George Blackburn away from Miami, as well as many of the players. Bo felt strange about this team divided; it was, as far as he was concerned, Miami against itself. Strangely, though, the closeness of the competition inspired Schembechler and his teammates to a 28–0 victory. That act of confronting someone so like himself was something Schembechler would experience over and over, growing to savor it as the true contest athletics has to offer and the defining measure of a coach.

After graduating from Miami, Schembechler was a graduate assistant on Woody's staff at Ohio State. But the Korean War led him on a loop through the South, from army duty in Alabama to coaching one year at Presbyterian College in South Carolina. He neared home in 1955 with an assistant position at Bowling Green under Doyt Perry—a Woody Hayes acolyte—where he stayed a year, then under Parseghian at Northwestern, where he remained from 1956 to 1957. He closed the circle the following year when he returned to Woody Hayes at Ohio State.

Along the way, Schembechler encountered the concept of going up against your own for a second time while he was at Bowling Green, when, in 1955, Bowling Green and Miami played for the Mid-American Conference championship in Oxford. Miami was, at that point in the season, undefeated. In the locker room prior to the game, head coach Perry called on Schembechler to address the Bowling Green players. The thrill of facing off with friends in the place where he had once played was almost too much for Schembechler. From his mouth came nothing but primordial grunts.

The Bowling Green players, bewitched by Schembechler's excitement, charged on the field. A defense constructed to surprise Miami staved off scoring. Miami won by a mere 7–0. "It was a helluva game," Schembechler remembers, thinking, no doubt, of the powerful experience of confronting himself.

Schembechler was acting as assistant to Woody Hayes when his old "Snow Bowl" compatriot John Pont left Miami for Yale. Schembechler considered closing another circle and returning to Miami. Because Miami had become so friendly to its former athletes, Schembechler was a natural for the position.

Hayes, though, had other ideas. "You'll be the next head coach of Ohio State."

"Gee, that's a great idea, Woody. How much longer are you gonna coach?"

"Three to five years."

Schembechler wisely went ahead and applied for the Miami job. After his Miami team won back-to-back Mid-American Conference championships in 1965 and 1966, larger universities took some notice of him. After the 1966 season, he was in the running to be Wisconsin's head coach, but Wisconsin, in the end, hired John Coatta. Unfortunately, in his first two seasons there Coatta didn't win a game.

Then, after the 1968 season, Bump Elliot, retiring from the head coaching position at Michigan, called Schembechler to take his place. Again, Schembechler was not the first choice, but names such as Ara Parseghian and Joe Paterno rejected offers. Schembechler acquired the position through either dumb luck or cleverly mapped destiny. It was the singular place for him to become the coach he wanted to be.

The reason: Michigan provided the best conduit back to Hayes. There, Schembechler was finally able to face off with the man who embodied his own best self, once a year. In November of 1969, Schembechler realized his dream; he and Hayes became equals.

That spring, Schembechler launched spring practice on a Michigan campus that was aflame with political activism. The old-fashioned, often overbearing manner that Schembechler learned from Hayes scarcely suited the "question authority" climate. Moreover, the previous head coach Bump Elliot had a mild demeanor. Elliot had run spring practice in a light-hearted manner, once a day, five days a week.

Not so Schembechler. The team worked out twice a day, seven days a week, with a long run on Sunday. He strode the field like a general, grabbing many a face mask to give a player a piece of his mind. At the outset of spring training, the team's roster contained 125 names. By the end of the week, it was trimmed back to 85. Schembechler established a motto for his thinning ranks: "Those Who Stay Will Be Champions."

The subtext of that seemingly general statement was quite specific. From the outset of the season, Schembechler defined the essential task: beat Ohio State.

The team exhibited the potential to challenge their foe. In the eight Saturdays prior to that end-of-the-season match,

Michigan lost only to Missouri, a nonleague team, a few days after Schembechler and his wife Millie had their first child, and later to Michigan State. A sound 31–20 defeat of Purdue—second in the Big Ten only to Ohio State—confirmed for Schembechler that his team had the talent to tackle Ohio State; a few weeks later, in a 51–6 drubbing of Iowa, he saw that his players had the desire. In the locker room after that game, the players chanted in unison *"Beat the Bucks,"* thumping the walls and smacking chairs until they were dizzy from the noise.

The reality outside Michigan's bubble of emotion was this: Ohio State's team was the finest in the school's history. Eighteen of twenty-two starters returned from the 1968 undefeated national championship team. For the first eight games of their 1969 season, they were unstoppable.

The morning of the game, Hayes began well before the clock started. When Schembechler went out on the field, Hayes had his team warming up on the Michigan side. When Schembechler pointed out the error, Hayes blithely herded his players to the other end of the field.

Somehow, Hayes gained the psychological edge he was after. On the first play of the game, the Ohio State quarterback, Rex Kern, gained twenty-five yards. On the next play, fullback Jim Otis ran for seven yards. But then, on the Michigan ten-yard line, Schembechler's defense stopped Ohio State on fourth and one.

Ohio State scored on their next drive, but missed the extra

point. The Michigan quarterback, Don Moorhead, threw three efficient passes to bring his team to the Ohio State three-yard line.

Schembechler called the play that made Hayes famous: fullback off tackle. It worked, and Michigan went ahead 7–6.

Unperturbed, Ohio State scored swiftly, but failed in their attempt for a two-point conversion. Moorhead answered with a series of first downs that took Michigan to the Ohio State thirty-three-yard line. The next play, tailback Billy Taylor carried the ball twenty-eight yards. Two plays later, Michigan led 14–12.

Michigan defensive back Barry Pierson returned a punt sixty yards to the Ohio State three-yard line. A quarterback sneak earned the touchdown. Toward the end of the first half, a Michigan interception of a Kern pass led to a field goal.

In the locker room during halftime, defensive coach Jim Young spoke the prophetic words: *"They will not score again."*

They didn't. Neither did Michigan... but they didn't need to.

When the game ended with a final score of 24–12, Schembechler's players hoisted him on their shoulders. He had grown as tall as Woody Hayes.

The victory over Ohio State sent Michigan to the Rose Bowl. The night before the game, Schembechler suffered a heart attack that hospitalized him. His demoralized players succumbed to USC 10–3.

In Schembechler's twenty seasons at Michigan, the Rose

Bowl invited his Michigan team to play ten times. They won just twice. The Rose Bowl, it seemed, was an afterthought, an inconsequential event that took place after the real competition was over. And all the games occurring prior to that contest were templates for the climax, with the visage of Ohio State a perpetual mask over other opponents. During the regular season, Schembechler was Hayes. He hollered, fumed, cajoled, and loved his players. Once, on the night before a game against a weak Northwestern squad, he studied a film of Northwestern's team and concluded his team was ill prepared for the matchup. He marched through the hotel, into the rooms of players and assistant coaches, waking some up, turning off televisions, yelling, coaxing, chiding, and encouraging so that his team, next day, was so prepared that they shut Northwestern down 69–0.

But each year, after the clock ran out on the Michigan–Ohio State game, Schembechler was without his mirror image across the field. As a result, he seemed to lose his sense of himself. At the Rose Bowl, there was no mirror image on the other side of the field. But time would circle around, fall would return, and Schembechler would begin intense preparation for his annual face-off with Hayes.

This way, Bo went for years without a losing season.

Ten years after Schembechler's first matchup with Hayes in 1969, another circle closed. When Michigan squared off against North Carolina in the Gator Bowl, Schembechler faced head coach Dick Crum, another Miami graduate, and assistants Denny Marcin and Jack Himebauch, both of whom Schembechler coached at Miami. They were two more sons who had joined the brotherhood.

A reporter who frequently covered Michigan games rode the elevator down from the press box after the game with the victorious Carolina staff, among them Marcin and Himebauch.

"They were laughing at you," the reporter later informed Schembechler.

Schembechler dismissed him. "Those kids played for me. You think they're not excited about beating me?"

He could empathize.

Whenever Schembechler and Hayes faced each other after that 1969 game, they each stayed on their own side of the fifty-yard line as they shook hands. Despite their history together, they spoke little. Their relationship was communicated during the game. Football was the language they spoke. Likewise, it was the system of symbols with which Schembechler connected to Sid Gillman, Ara Parseghian, Denny Marcin, and Jack Himebauch.

Despite the myriad circles football offered Schembechler, there was no closure more satisfying than the student surpassing the teacher. Pont must have felt it when his Indiana team defeated Ara Parseghian's Northwestern squad; and Bill Mallory, another Miami graduate, must have savored that pleasure when his own Indiana defeated Hayes's Buckeyes. Really, as in all these instances, Schembechler and Hayes's relationship offered a type of competition that allowed both to be their best selves. They had the opportunity to renew those best selves on a November Saturday ten years in a row. More satisfaction for Schembechler: he won the series 5–4–1. The margin of victory was slim, but what else could be expected from a battle of equals?

7

The Coach and the Man

Carm Cozza has always divided his time between worlds: baseball and football, academics and athletics, men and women, small town and a university that some think is the center of the cosmos.

Cozza was born in Parma, Ohio, ten miles from Cleveland. The proximity to that city gave him little more than an awareness of the Cleveland Indians; his setting was bucolic, the family life idyllic. Chickens roamed the yard, and vines produced grapes for homemade wine.

The only boy among five children and the youngest, Cozza led a charmed youth. He was raised by his sisters, Pat, Theresa, Josephine, and Ange. Because they were all substantially older than he, they shared with their mother the raising of their little brother, often pampering him. Ange bought him his first car and forged the permission slip Cozza needed to try out for his high school football team.

For Cozza, one sports season bled into the next. In the summertime, he threw apples at the house. Time passed breezily, Cozza received accolades as a high school athlete, then colleges came knocking. They all wanted him to play football. With the scholarships they offered, Cozza would become the first in his family to attend college. His father turned up his nose at football, but he was certainly sold on the idea of a scholarship. Cozza accepted the one offered by Miami, and became teammates with John Pont and Bo Schembechler. His coach, Woody Hayes, made Cozza mentally tough. The first time he touched the football for Miami, as a sophomore, he bobbled a punt, but, out of fear of what Hayes might do to him, managed to pick it back up and run it for a touchdown.

But Cozza loved baseball first, loved playing it most. Though he was a versatile member of Miami's football team, playing three positions, among them quarterback, he was most comfortable throwing a baseball. After graduating, he signed on with the Cleveland Indians franchise; after he married his childhood sweetheart (John Pont was his best man), he moved to Cedar Rapids, Iowa, to play for the Indians farm team. In the off-season, he took graduate courses and coached high school sports, but he remained loyal to the dreams.

Jean, his wife, was someone Cozza had known his whole life. She, too, loved baseball, and the two of them, with another friend, would put on uniforms and play baseball in the dusty road.

But the birth of their first two daughters, Chris and Kathy, altered his perception of himself as an athlete. In 1956, his old

Miami roommate John Pont, just named head coach at their alma mater, offered Cozza a full-time position as head of the freshmen program. In light of his daughters, Cozza couldn't refuse the stability.

Once Cozza stepped inside the world of football, he couldn't leave. He stayed at Miami with Pont for seven seasons, then moved with Pont to Yale along with the bulk of the Miami staff in 1963. At the time, Cozza was disappointed by the move. He had dreamed of manning the helm of his alma mater.

It all worked out for Cozza soon enough. In 1965, when Pont moved to Indiana, Cozza stayed in New Haven to be head coach. Three years later, Pont's younger brother Richard joined Cozza's staff at Yale, keeping the brotherhood intact.

Cozza lost the opening game of his head-coaching career to the University of Connecticut, Yale's first loss against an in-state opponent since 1935. A loss three weeks later to Columbia was underscored by an embarrassing, failed attempt to integrate the worlds of men and women. In a symbolic effort to push Yale toward coeducation, the football team adopted eight cheerleaders from Connecticut College for Women. Worse than the 21–7 loss for Yale was the *New York Times* headline: "8 Girl Cheerleaders Shout in Vain for Elis to Hold 'Em." The cheerleaders were dismissed.

Cozza had to wait till the 1967 season to reconcile his divided worlds. In 1966, two great players, both recruited by Cozza, took the field, and their differences would eventually add up to a sum of victory.

Brian Dowling and Calvin Hill were as disparate as Cozza's

two sides. The former was affluent, the other the son of an unemployed construction worker. Dowling hailed from Ohio, where Cozza had his roots, and Hill, like Cozza, made his way through school on scholarships. They were both, as Cozza was, quarterbacks.

Dowling was tall, quick, smart. As a quarterback in junior high and then at St. Ignatius High School in Cleveland, Dowling had never played in a losing football game. He was a standout in several other sports; as a result, he received one hundred scholarship offers. Brian turned them all down. His father, a Youngstown Sheet and Tube Company executive, could foot the bill.

Hill had grown up in Baltimore. He took a step closer to Yale when he transferred to Riverdale Country School in New York on a scholarship designated for a black student. Like Dowling, he was a high school quarterback who had never lost a game.

During his first season, 1965, freshman coach Harry Jacunski, the eighth man of the Seven Blocks of Granite that made Fordham's 1936 team legendary, pegged Dowling as quarterback and Hill as running back. His intuition proved to be more fortuitous than he could have imagined; Hill was a natural. In one game in that first season, he ran for four touchdowns.

The next year on varsity, Dowling at quarterback and Hill at his new position rectified the previous year's loss to the University of Connecticut, stopping them cold in a 16–0 victory. Dowling, though, was injured the next week in a loss to

Rutgers, and missed the rest of the season. The season ended with a record of 4–5, but with Cozza looking forward to a healthy quarterback for 1967.

Cozza's ambition for Dowling was high; so was his affection. The same day that Dowling injured his leg, Cozza learned that Dowling's father had passed away in Cleveland. As soon as Cozza heard the news, he was on his way to Dowling's room, where he knew the player was resting.

A few days later, Cozza left game preparation to his assistant coaches and joined Dowling and his family at the funeral, offering his paternal support to fill the void.

In one world Cozza had his athletes. In another, he had three daughters, the loveliest creatures in the Yale Bowl, not only because of their faces, but because of the passion with which they watched their father. With their mother, Jean, they never missed a game, home or away. Cozza brought players to his home, where they joked and flirted with the girls. The athletes coddled the girls, while the girls told little stories to entertain. Dick Jauron often serenaded them with his guitar. Dave Butz once draped his jacket over Kathy, and the little giggling girl was swallowed whole.

As often as he could, Cozza liked to drive his daughters to school in Orange, Connecticut, chatting with them about the school days behind and ahead. Those moments of connection with daughters and with Dowling made him a better coach.

Despite the fact that Dowling fractured his wrist during a practice in the early part of the 1967 season, causing a Yale loss in the first game against Holy Cross, Dowling sat out only one game and then returned to join Hill, driving the team along a sixteen-win streak that stretched into the 1968 season. The Dowling-Hill combination generated resounding victories, among them the 1967 demolition of Dartmouth by a score of 56–15, the highest score Yale reached in a game in over thirty years. The play that epitomized the magic of the two occurred during the 29–7 win over Princeton. The first Yale touchdown began as a handoff from Dowling to Hill, who bounced right to give Dowling time to run downfield, where Hill hit him with a sixty-yard pass.

Cozza's team emerged as Ivy League champions and continued to play with athleticism and commitment into the 1968 season, cruising to a second championship in a row. Added to Cozza's stable of talent that year was a new offensive backfield coach, Richard Pont, whose gentle touch would spark new fire in Calvin Hill.

Harvard, though, in handling their opponents, was having an equally easy time of it. When they met in Harvard stadium on November 23, 1968, both teams were undefeated.

In the second quarter, the Dowling-Hill duo appeared unstoppable. Dowling secured one touchdown on a three-yard run; two Dowling passes led to touchdowns, one to Hill, who, with that score, became Yale's all-time high point earner. Harvard's second-string quarterback managed a completion for a touchdown, but Harvard couldn't execute the extra point kick. At the half, Yale led 21–6.

Though Harvard scored once in the third quarter, the crowd on the Yale side of the stadium began celebrating when, from the five-yard line, Dowling ran an option around the corner to widen the gap of the score to 29–13. Soon after, again deep in Harvard territory, Yale threatened to increase the margin again, but a Yale receiver fumbled a Dowling pass.

The Harvard second-string quarterback, Frank Champi, reentered the game and spun a series of mistakes, some by Yale, some by himself, into gold. First, he fumbled, but one of his linemen recovered and carried the ball to the Yale fifteen. Then Champi dashed around, unable to find a receiver, losing yardage, breaking free of many a tackle before he found an open man, who scored. A call against Yale for pass interference gave Harvard two chances at a two-point conversion; the second was successful, tightening the score to 29–21 with forty-two seconds left in the game.

After Harvard recovered their onside kick and Yale was penalized fifteen yards for a face-mask violation, Harvard found themselves in a sweet position: first down on the Yale twenty-yard line. The Yale fans were stunned and the Harvard fans ebullient.

Amid the chaos, Dowling and Hill approached Cozza. They requested that they be put in on defense. Cozza hesitated; he could use them at safety and defensive back.

But he didn't hesitate for long. Cozza told his star players: "We would destroy two young men if we took them out now."

Harvard scored a touchdown and a two-point conversion,

ending the game in a 29–29 tie. For Harvard fans, this was an uplifting victory; for Yale, it was bitter defeat.

Yale was forced to share the Ivy League crown with Harvard—but two young men were spared destruction. Was Cozza's decision that of a coach or a man?

Certainly the latter. Cozza was a coach, but he was also a man who loved all his kids. On a steamy August afternoon in 1968, the players were hangdog throughout practice. Cozza stormed away from the field. A few minutes later, he returned in the passenger seat of an ice-cream truck. The players lined up for their ice cream. Cozza picked up the tab.

His team won the Ivy League title again in 1969, sharing it with Dartmouth, then won or tied for the championship four times in the seventies. That coaching success might be one reason Cozza never left New Haven.

Another reason, though, might be the women in his life. During his thirty-two years at Yale, Cozza received two job offers from other colleges, one to be head coach, one athletic director. On one of those occasions, Cozza thought seriously about moving. When he brought the subject up with his family, his daughter Kathy immediately burst into tears. Cozza was a man. How could he resist his little girl?

He stayed beside his family; he stayed beside his players. Dick Jauron once told the following story: "In my senior year I ran eighty-seven yards against Columbia for a touchdown, and Coach ran alongside down the sidelines and hugged me in the end zone. He was such a great athlete, I wouldn't have been surprised if he'd beaten me!"

Cozza's brilliance was that he could let one of his worlds inform the other so easily. Intelligence might appear to some to be analysis, breaking things down, differentiating between unlike parts. Far more challenging, though, is to find the similarity of opposites. How is an orange like an apple? How is Brian Dowling like Calvin Hill? How is Cozza the coach like Cozza the man? They are the same, and because they are, Cozza was a champion.

8

Loyalty

In 1952, when Bill Mallory was attending high school in Sandusky, Ohio, his parents moved to Hillsboro, in another part of the state. Young Mallory elected to stay in Sandusky, living with family friends so he could complete his senior year of football. Many years later, in 1980, when Mallory accepted the head coaching position at Northern Illinois, the high school coach in Boulder tried to pursuade Mallory to allow his son Mike to do as he had done in 1952, to finish his senior year of football at the high school to which he had become loyal, away from his family.

Without hesitation, Mallory took his son to De Kalb, Illinois, along with him, his wife, and his other children. Football, he had learned, should not divide families. It should bring them together.

The football blood in Mallory's family flowed from Guy Mallory, Bill's father, who coached high school ball at two schools outside of Delaware, Ohio. That football blood pulsed in the veins of his sons. Bill played for Miami of Ohio, where he was coached by Ara Parseghian and John Pont. He was followed, systematically, by his younger brothers, Tom and Dave, creating a ten-year span of Mallory time for Miami football.

Loyalty doesn't always mean playing for the same team, however. By the time Dave was in the position of middle linebacker for Bo Schembechler's Miami team, older brother Bill had landed a position as Doyt Perry's assistant at Bowling Green. During the game, Miami ran an unusual defense that pushed the play out of bounds. Though the whistle blew, Dave continued his route and smacked into the ball carrier for a late hit.

"Call it, call it, call it," Bill bellowed at the refs from the Bowling Green sideline. Dave leaped to his feet, confronted his brother, and offered him a few choice words.

To any of the Mallorys, loyalty didn't mean complacency. It meant toughness and honesty in playing the game of football.

Though the three sons of Guy Mallory excelled in college football, only Bill followed his father and his Miami cohorts into coaching. Tom became an orthopedic surgeon and Dave a dentist, both practicing in Ohio. Nevertheless, despite their career moves, football factored into the younger brothers' lives, on one notable occasion in relation to Bill's oldest son, Mike.

Mike was heavily recruited by high-power programs. An Ohio State assistant coach, intent on wooing Mike, implemented his methods of persuasion at Uncle Dave Mallory's dentist office in Loudonville, Ohio. During the discussion, he admired a photo of Dave's family, remarking particularly on Dave's son. At that point, Dave was able to inform the Ohio State recruiter that his son's name was Bo.

The fellow from Ohio State knew there was no chance of bringing a Mallory to Columbus. Mike chose Ann Arbor as his temple and Schembechler as his football priest.

Mike's younger brothers, Doug and Curt, also played for the Mallorys' loyal friend at Michigan, Schembechler. They liked to keep things in the family.

As time's mirror to Guy Mallory's offspring, all three of Bill Mallory's sons played football. Their father did his best to watch them play when they were young. He was often able to catch the first half of a Friday game before he needed to return to work. He stood outside the fence of his sons' games for long enough to feel that victory was inevitable; then he drove away.

Mallory's early coaching career kept him tight in the fold of his other family, the Miami brotherhood. He was assistant to Doyt Perry at Bowling Green, to Carm Cozza at Yale, and to Woody Hayes at Ohio State, following on the heels of Bo Schembechler on two of those occasions. Mallory's loyalty to Schembechler emerged because they had been molded by the same minds.

Though Hayes threw a film projector at Mallory on one occasion, Mallory, like Schembechler, studied him most closely for a method of coaching. Hayes, he felt, hit on the essential goal of a college athletic program: education. By witnessing Hayes as he badgered players to study, to finish school, to pursue graduate work, to try again when they failed on any level, Mallory learned how to keep vigil over his athletes' academic progress. Throughout his career, he held meetings with advisors, grilled tutors, called parents to apprise them of difficulties, and frequently sat a wayward young man down in his office for a stern lecture about what football was *really* about.

Mallory had a chair in his office that players on the sly called the "Hot Seat." It was the site of many a finger wagging, mostly about grades, but sometimes addressing such disparate topics as preparation for a job interview or politeness to the secretaries in the football office.

Though Mallory credits Hayes for imparting these values to him, really they belonged to all the other Miami men with whom he had contact. He couldn't help but adopt them. As a result, that Mallory received the head coaching position at Miami in 1969 after Schembechler moved to Michigan seemed more natural than childbirth.

In his first few seasons, from 1969 to 1972, Mallory's teams breezed by nonconference opponents, but struggled with Mid-American opposition. In 1973, though, in the manner of all his mentors, Mallory guided his Miami team to the best record in the school's history. The team was led by Bob

Hitchens, who eclipsed Mallory's former coach John Pont in the running game, concluding the season as Miami's all-time leader in rushing and scoring. Victories over high-power teams like Purdue and Paul Dietzel's South Carolina squad enhanced Miami's sweep of the Mid-American Conference, earning them a bid to the Tangerine Bowl to face Florida. Prior to the game, the Florida team conveyed their contempt for their northern opponents in covert ways that trickled up to Oxford. Mallory sent back the simple message, "You tell 'em we're gonna be there." Miami's pride on the line, the players dealt Florida a 16–7 loss.

With that victory came the opportunity that Mallory had anticipated, that he felt was expected of a Miami coach, to leap into the limelight as the head of a major program.

Mallory's wife anticipated the move, too. She had become acclimated to the idea. When Mallory drove his wife Ellie from Columbus to Oxford in a Volkswagen bug, she was pregnant with their youngest son, Curt. It was a ride so uncomfortable that, later on, any move, any rockiness she experienced watching her husband and her son's games, year in and year out, became second nature.

Football was not always so natural to her. When Bill and Ellie were first dating, they had the rare opportunity of attending a game together. At one point during the game, the scoreboard read, DOWN: 2, and Ellie was incredulous. "Down two?" she queried. "I think there are at least eight fellas on the field."

While Bill and Ellie were students at Miami, she elected to sell cider during the games. After she and Bill were married, though, Ellie learned to watch football. When her sons were old enough to play in Colorado and then Illinois, she would often find herself on three-day football binges—junior high, high school, and her husband's college games. She was required to keep stats of the games or portions of games that her husband missed to report to him when he came home that night. Ellie became at least as consumed by football as her husband was. Once, while Mallory led the program at the University of Colorado, Ellie added a fourth football game to her usual gridiron bender: she sat in Mile High Stadium while the Denver Broncos played in a Sunday matchup. She was so glutted with football that, during the game, she fell fast asleep.

Perhaps Colorado did her in: the thin air, the exhaustive demands. Though Mallory always liked best the place where he was and had no problems shaking the dust from his feet to move on; though he led a charmed football career, wined and dined to accept each position he took; though that welcoming allowed him, for the most part, to regard Oxford, Boulder, De Kalb, and Bloomington as his homes, really Colorado was too far from Ohio. He, likewise, was too far from Colorado. Despite invitations to the Bluebonnet Bowl in 1975, in which Colorado battled Texas and lost, 38–21, and to the Orange Bowl in 1977, in which Colorado fell to Ohio State 27–10 in one of the last games of Woody Hayes's glorious reign; despite, that same year, driving to a Big Eight title, the university was uncommitted to Mallory, and he was uncomfortable with it. They let him go.

Happily, a call requesting that Mallory assume the head coaching position at Northern Illinois in 1980 allowed him to go home.

Northern Illinois had joined the Mid-American Conference in 1973, but struggled against the talent of teams such as Miami and Bowling Green. In this familiar territory, Mallory understood everything he needed to do. He turned the program around, taking them, in 1983, to an undefeated season, a Mid-American Conference championship, and a postseason bowl game.

After the victory in that game, the California Bowl, programs more high profile than Northern Illinois once again turned their gaze to Mallory. Luckily, one was just down the road, both in distance and in spirit: his old coach John Pont's former stomping grounds, Indiana University.

A more subtle but perhaps greater success, personally, that Mallory constructed at Northern Illinois was his restructuring of a coach's day. Though the coaches who mentored him— particularly Woody Hayes and Doyt Perry—worked incessant hours to achieve their success, Mallory suspected that he could elevate effort and loyalty from his staff if he sent them home to their families more often. After reading studies on time management, he restructured the staff's workday, gathering them as early as 6:30 in the morning so that they could, at the end of the day, enjoy dinner with their families. In addition, all were free on Friday and Sunday mornings. Mallory enforced this system by the adherence to what became known as "Mallory Time": when he said 6:30, he really meant 6:25. Assistants and players alike knew never to attempt walking through a door after Mallory did; they would find it locked. Mallory was never late, nor would he ever consider unlocking the door.

He carried his healthy, thoughtful attitude toward coaches and toward players to Indiana, a team that had only three winning seasons between John Pont's 1967 Rose Bowl team and Mallory's arrival. In three years, though, Mallory improved Indiana's record from 0–11 in 1984, to 4–7 in 1985, to 6–6 in 1986, with an invitation to the All-American Bowl. His touch, both firm and gentle, had placed his team in a promising position in 1987. The mantra around the locker room was, "It's happening." But when it started to happen, when Indiana won three of their first four games, no one took much notice.

Like their coach, Indiana football players were not football behemoths manufactured by a football machine. At their best, they were giant killers. Luckily, the Big Ten offered many giants for them to slay.

For example, on October 10, 1987, Indiana faced Ohio State, a team they had not been able to beat for thirty-five years. In the gladiatorial arena of Ohio Stadium, Indiana held their opponents to a score of 10–10 at the half. Early in the fourth quarter, the Ohio State defense had Indiana backed against a wall on their own three-yard line. It looked as if David would succumb to Goliath. At that point, the Indiana quarterback, sophomore Dave Schnell, in his first varsity season, took action. He gestured to the fans in the stadium to make them louder. They roared in response. Mallory couldn't believe the young player's nerve, and was skeptical of its wisdom. But then, when Schnell ran the option and took off down the field, moving the Indiana offense into safer territory, the crowd grew quiet with awe. David had prevailed.

The Indiana defense played their role as well, holding Ohio State to ten rushing yards in the second half. Indiana won resoundingly, 31–10.

For the first time in years, Indiana earned a national ranking, coming in at number eighteen. The following week they held off Minnesota, and then triumphed over Bo Schembechler's Michigan squad, whom they had not defeated in fifteen years. As they approached the end of the season, they shared the leadership in the Big Ten with Michigan State, another David-like program. They had not been to the Rose Bowl since 1967.

Two weeks before the matchup with Michigan State, the worst thing that can happen to any team, let alone a low-profile program, occurred: a key player couldn't play. Dave Schnell had an emergency appendectomy. The second-string quarterback, Dave Kramme, could not execute, and Michigan State vehemently claimed their trip to the Rose Bowl with a score of 27–3.

At the end of the game, Mallory went straight to the Michigan State locker room. Quieting the celebration for a moment, he addressed the team. "You represent the Big Ten in the Rose Bowl," Mallory said. "You have the challenge and the responsibility to win it for the Big Ten."

For Mallory, football, in the end, was about loyalty, not opposition.

During the years Mallory coached Indiana, his players lined up facing his sons on the Michigan team. The confrontation was troublesome only because of media attention. Their mother instructed them, "You don't pick or scratch anything, because the cameras will be on you." Otherwise, father and sons simply played football, with Michigan winning all years but 1987. Mallory could only be proud. He took on Curt and Mike as graduate assistants at Indiana, so they could, for a bit, stand on their father's side of the field before moving on to full-time positions.

In 1995, after a season as a student coach at Michigan and two as a graduate assistant at Indiana, Curt was hired to his first full-time college stint, as linebacker coach at Ball State. When he was preparing his new team to face Miami in the opening game of the season, Curt called up his father to make sure he'd be in attendance.

"We'll be sitting in the Miami press box," Mallory admitted. He then informed his son that he would be honored at halftime by his alma mater for his contributions to Miami athletics.

"Oh no," exclaimed Curt. "Not my first game."

Again in 1995 Mallory was lauded by the opposing team against which his son Curt was coaching, and for which his son Mike served as defensive coordinator. It was the Northern Illinois–Ball State game, and the two sons felt the presence of their father. While the halftime crowd applauded Mallory and his entire 1983 Northern Illinois squad, which had been Mid-American Conference and California Bowl champions, sons Mike and Curt both watched. When Mallory first heard over the phone that he would be honored under those circumstances, in front of both sons, he had his own opportunity to exclaim, "Oh, no!"

But he went to receive his accolades. He knew, as his sons did, that you often have to hand the spotlight over to family.

Doug, who played defensive back at Michigan, made the University of Maryland his home. Though he was far from familiar digs, he worked under one of his father's former Indiana assistants: Elliot Uzelac. Recently, though, he brought his own flesh and blood there: Mike joined the staff early in 2000.

Some families can't seem to stay apart for very long. Even though Mallory's sons are now standing on sidelines other than their father's, really, they never left home. With their father, they are on one side, rooting for one ideal: tough, honest, Ohio-bred football.

9

Luck

In 1953, a high school senior named Don Nehlen visited Miami of Ohio, hoping to play, among other sports, football. Just as Sid Gillman turned away John Pont back in 1947, head coach Ara Parseghian promptly turned Nehlen away. The boy, Parseghian thought, just wasn't big enough. He hadn't learned yet that Ohio boys are as big as they want to be.

Nehlen made no bones about who he was. He was "Bonesy," the skinniest kid on Canton Lincoln's football, basketball, and baseball rosters and also the luckiest. He knew about luck. Nehlen's parents were serious poker players. From them, Nehlen inherited the notion that a gamble is not a fling with chance, but rather a highly calculated venture. Hard work, they would teach him, keeps the variables in check.

At first, he let others gamble on him. The summer before his junior year, a starry-eyed Nehlen was invited to play third base for the Timken Roller Bearing Company's Class A Industrial League team. Along with that came a summer job at the plant.

Luck made him a little spoiled. His older sister Jane reported that he was a "sissy" when he was younger, sucking on his bottle till he was five years old and perpetually begging her for canned milk, water, and sugar. In light of his success in baseball, he nearly quit football. But the high school coach begged him to stick it out. As it turned out, at quarterback his senior year, Nehlen led Canton Lincoln to the coveted city championship.

He must have figured all those gamblers knew what they were doing, so he gambled on himself.

Luckily, up the road from Miami of Ohio is its slightly less glamorous but equally persistent rival, Bowling Green State University. In the fall of 1954, two years after my father graduated, Nehlen drove onto campus in his 1950 Pontiac, with reservations. His first love was baseball, and his 5'11", 140-pound frame was, perhaps, better suited for it. When Nehlen quit his job at the Timken Roller Bearing Company—a place in which he was being groomed for advancement—his boss, head of engineering Earl Schreiber, took a good look at him.

"You're going to play college football?"

"Yes, sir. I'm going to make a stab at it."

Schreiber couldn't hold back his laughter.

But in Ohio, you can't maintain reservations about football, especially when Doyt Perry becomes your coach, as he did at

Bowling Green in 1955, Nehlen's first year of eligibility. Perry took on a rocky program that had accumulated a mere three wins in the previous two seasons. Perry added another challenge to his plate: he chose to start at quarterback the kid so skinny he went by the nicknames "Bones" and "Bonesy." Desperate to gain some girth, Nehlen maintained a job in the student cafeteria, opening juice cans at five o'clock in the morning. Afterward, he was allowed to eat all the breakfast he could hold. Usually, he downed enough for two or three people.

When Perry first set eyes on Nehlen, he assumed that Nehlen didn't belong and shouted at him to leave. But Perry was a bit of a gambler, too, like Nehlen's family. He took no chances in his style of play—which challenged Woody Hayes's "three yards and a cloud of dust" philosophy for conservatism. He took all his risks with people.

He so believed in Nehlen, girth or no, he ordered him to quit that job in the cafeteria, regardless of its caloric benefits, so that he could sleep a little later.

Meanwhile, down in Oxford, the players were living high on the hog under the guidance of Ara Parseghian in his final Miami season. They stormed past their competitors, amassing seven wins and no losses before confronting Bowling Green. Parseghian's team, ranked tenth in the country, overcame Bowling Green by a mere 7–0.

The next year, Bowling Green was 8–0–1 when they again faced Miami. Miami had been leading the game by a 7–0 score when Bowling Green blocked a Miami punt. The result was a touchdown and extra point for Bowling Green, making it 7–7, the final score of the game. The tie cost Miami the Mid-American Conference championship title, which they had held during both years of Parseghian's reign. What was a tremendous embarrassment for new Miami coach John Pont made a deep impression on Nehlen. He'd been able to keep the giants at bay.

"In those days, the guys who walked on water were Ara Parseghian and John Pont," said Nehlen.

Though Nehlen wasn't playing for Parseghian or Pont, Perry was an awfully close approximation, created out of the same Ohio mold. Because Perry was clearly doing something right, Nehlen studied his coach. He discovered that the coaching staff remained in their trailerlike office outside the stadium deep into the night. Nehlen couldn't help but wonder what Perry and his staff did in there. Through observing their actions, he found that they were studying football: they were working through plays.

Nehlen followed suit. Like Perry, he committed all his time and energy to understanding the patterns and nuances of the game. When one freshman football player first met him, Nehlen appeared to be studying. Because it was the beginning of the school year, the freshman asked the older player what he was doing. It turns out he was memorizing the entire football rule book, carefully underlining the sanctions that specifically affected quarterbacks.

In Nehlen's three years at starting quarterback, his team lost only twice. The first was that 1955 loss to Parseghian's Miami squad. Then in 1956, the team charged through its Mid-American Conference schedule, ultimately securing the league championship with a resounding 41–27 win over Ohio University. Throughout the season, but most notably in that final game, Nehlen facilitated the crucial plays. He completed eight of fifteen passes for 151 yards, and scored on a nine-yard run.

When, in 1957, Miami and Bowling Green faced each other again, they were both undefeated. In a moment of déjà vu, the score at the half was tied 7–7. Pont took his team into the locker room and fired up his players. Perhaps that's why the game ended in his favor, 13–7. Perhaps, though, Nehlen played a role. While on defense, he moved up from his safety position to tackle a Miami runner. When he made the hit, the strap protecting his face broke from his helmet and pierced him in the eye. He was out for the rest of the game.

But he played the following week in a game against Ohio University that ended in a 7–7 tie.

People cite Doyt Perry's record at Bowling Green—77–11–5—as testimony to a greatness surpassed by few coaches. But Perry himself dismisses such accolades. He believes he couldn't have done it without Nehlen.

The Hollywood glamour of an Ara Parseghian or a Paul Dietzel belies the truth of football: it is a sport so complex that it overwhelms even itself; both coaches and players grunt, sweat, and stumble beneath the bulk of its demands. Nowhere is that burden made lighter by history or by money, not South Bend, not Columbus, not Canton, not Massillon. Football always bears down with its full weight.

Perry was not glamorous. To coach, he donned old brown pants, a T-shirt, and a weather-beaten baseball cap. In that workingman's garb, he rolled the dice with his players.

But, really, it requires two such gamblers to lift a dusty program like that at Bowling Green to the heights of success and public interest.

And for Nehlen, life was always a gamble. After college, with neither money nor a job, he married his childhood sweetheart Merry Ann Chopson, holding a bridal dance designed to pay for itself. Friends and family tossed coins and bills into a metal bucket, ostensibly to dance with Merry Ann, but really to offer the newlyweds a financial start. The four hundred dollars in the pail amply paid for their Niagara Falls honeymoon.

For years, Nehlen continued to gamble. In his first position, at perennial underdog Canton South High School, which hadn't posted a winning season in eight years, he turned the program around so that it could hold its own with Canton McKinley and Massillon. He passed up an opportunity to assist Woody Hayes at Ohio State, choosing instead to assist Doyt Perry's successor at Bowling Green because Perry (who had moved on to become athletic director) told Nehlen he might get a shot at the head coaching position if it came open. In 1968, he took the helm at his alma mater.

Any gambler is going to come up against the percentages: one can't always win. Though Nehlen had just one losing season at Bowling Green, in 1970, the 2–6–1 record was devastating enough to leave a sour taste in the mouth of fans and critics alike. Moreover, for Nehlen, the personal circumstances that eroded his ability to perform proved to be something he, and his family, would live with forever.

His son Danny, a ten-year-old who loved football as much as his father did, was missing a vertebra. After extensive surgery, Danny was immobilized for six weeks and wore a brace for six months; when it was removed, he needed to relearn walking. Danny reclaimed that ability but was never again able to pursue athletics.

What happens at home happens on the field, especially for a man as committed as Nehlen. That year, on the field, and off, nothing seemed to go right.

Though the 39–22–2 record of the following six years was respectable, Nehlen was more upset for his assistant coaches than for himself when the staff was let go. He could find comedy only when his daughter Vicki wondered aloud, "Why does everyone hate you?" Luckily, another Doyt Perry acolyte invited Nehlen to join his staff as an assistant: Bo Schembechler at Michigan.

Nehlen's three years in Ann Arbor revived his faith in football and his commitment to excellence so completely that he had the courage to forge ahead with the greatest gamble of his professional life, assuming the head coaching position at the University of West Virginia.

The situation could be no worse in Morgantown, a town unmarred by glamour.

By 1979, the team, the university, even the state had become accustomed to defeat. The annual contest with Pittsburgh mustered some excitement on the field and in the stands, but that spirit hibernated the rest of the season. Nehlen saw the program as a gamble like all the others he had played and won.

To resurrect it, he first chose to change the team's image: he designed new uniforms, pitching an austere blue-and-white combination that made the mountaineers strangely resemble Penn State, and adopting the helmet with the flying "WV."

Some of the cards he inherited were more than playable. First of all, the university had committed itself to constructing a new stadium with artificial turf and 50,000 seats, nearly twice as many as the old Mountaineer Field held.

On September 6, 1980, when Nehlen's team took on its first opponent, Cincinnati, the newly completed stadium overflowed with 50,150 fans, among them John Denver and Governor Rockefeller.

Visually, the players no longer resembled those on the teams that lost. They looked like Don Nehlen's creation. Nevertheless, Nehlen later admitted to feeling the weight of tremendous pressure. That Cincinnati scored first early in the game on a forty-five-yard field goal didn't help matters. Regardless, he gained some confidence as the game progressed from another card he had inherited, a quarterback still in his junior year with the auspicious name of Luck.

Oliver Luck completed ten of fifteen passes for 138 yards and two touchdowns, guiding a final 41–27 victory over Cincinnati.

Though that 1980 season closed with a 6–6 record, Luck was planning to stick around for another year... and that doesn't just mean Oliver.

The bottom line with West Virginia football, as Nehlen knew, was that those who filled the uniforms were the real gamble. Locale was the variable most difficult to control. "When you fly over West Virginia, you see treetops," Nehlen once said. "When you fly over Ohio, you see rooftops. There are a lot more football players under roofs than under trees." So multisport athletes, walk-ons, and transfers were the perpetual (if unpredictable) source of talent. A seasoned gambler plays whatever cards he's dealt.

In the spring of 1981, Luck again smiled on Nehlen. A Pennsylvania native named Jeff Hostetler chose to leave his position as second-string quarterback on Penn State's team to join West Virginia's ranks. With him, Nehlen held quite a hand.

Judging by appearances, Hostetler's destiny was to be a Nittany Lion. His older brothers Doug and Ron were linebackers for Joe Paterno—both converts from quarterback. One senses that the same fate might have befallen Jeff.

Paterno did not turn Hostetler away, as Parseghian had once done to Nehlen. That he started Todd Blackledge was hardly arbitrary. Not only did Blackledge have the talent to carry Penn State to the 1982 national championship, he came from football stock with which Nehlen could claim kinship. His father played for Bowling Green just following Nehlen's tenure there and went on to coach with him at Canton South.

Nevertheless, it was Hostetler who found himself at the less glamorous school down the road a piece, coached by the embodiment of Doyt Perry.

Hostetler played backup to Luck in 1981, when the team finished the season 9–3, seventeenth in the national rankings, and victorious in its postseason Peach Bowl game against Florida.

Then Hostetler moved in to fill Luck's shoes in the 1982 season opener against Oklahoma.

The largest crowd in the school's history (75,008) assembled in Oklahoma Stadium in Norman. To its delight, Oklahoma took an early 14–0 lead. Then Hostetler rallied West Virginia to bring them to a 27–27 tie. In the fourth quarter, he led two more scoring drives to which Oklahoma could not respond. He didn't throw a single interception, despite the merciless onslaught of the Oklahoma defense.

That game thrust West Virginia into the national limelight. They remained in the top-twenty rankings during the next two seasons, capping off Hostetler's college career with a 20–16 victory over Kentucky in the Bluebonnet Bowl.

After the '82 Oklahoma game, a trainer wrote on the injury report next to Hostetler's name simply: "body." That's the sacrifice you make when you play or coach West Virginia football. You bet the farm, then you fight to keep it. Hostetler never ceased in his labors. In the summertime, he worked a West Virginia coal tipple; during the school year, he worked for grades that earned him nomination for a Rhodes Scholarship. Where the Rhodes committee missed out, the New York Giants scored big, drafting a player who would, in 1990, win them the Super Bowl.

But who really won in this round of the great poker game that is West Virginia football? I say Nehlen: he gained a son-in-law. When Hostetler married Nehlen's daughter Vicki, she didn't think much of football, but Hostetler brought her around. Another win for Nehlen's side.

Morgantown became an Ohio enclave in the Appalachian mountains. But, Nehlen would find in the years to come, it wasn't easy to keep the spirit of Ohio alive beyond its borders. It was a struggle because he was too far away from the heart of Ohio football: his coaching brethren.

SIR SIDNEY RULES
Sid Gillman called the plays, and changed the way coaches thought about them. Bill Walsh, among others, credits him as the father of the West Coast Offense. *University of Cincinnati archives*

BEST OF THE WEST
Chicago Bears coach George Halas must have been relieved that his 1963 NFL championship team didn't have to face Sid Gillman's San Diego Chargers, the AFL champs, a team Halas believed to be the best in the country that year. *Chance Brockway*

BLAME IT ON THE WEATHER
The "Blizzard Bowl" of 1950 in Columbus,
in which Wes Fesler's Ohio State team
lost to Michigan, cost Fesler his job...
and ushered in the era of Woody Hayes.
Photo courtesy of Bentley Historical Library,
University of Michigan

THE TEN-YEAR WAR Bo's and Woody's teams went at it on the field, but between the two there was a relationship of deepest respect and affection. Bo won the war, 5-4-1, the slim victory you might expect from a battle of equals. *Chance Brockway*

GO OUT FIGHTIN' Every detail mattered to Woody Hayes, from the punctuality of his players to the fitness level of his coaches to the passionate delivery of the Ohio State fight song. *Photos reprinted with permission of the* Columbus Dispatch

MEETING OF THE MINDS
No one was tougher than Woody Hayes,
except, perhaps, Bear Bryant.
Chance Brockway

PROMISES TO KEEP
Ara Parseghian vowed to
bring national championships
to Notre Dame ... and he did,
twice, in 1966 and 1973.
Chance Brockway

COACH OF THE CENTURY After receiving Coach of the Year honors in 1967, John Pont took Indiana to its only Rose Bowl on January 1, 1968. *Chance Brockway*

FATHER FIGURE
Pont tried to let his
players feel they were
on equal footing with
their coach. *Indiana*
University Archives
(#65-1180-27)

CLOSE BUT NO CIGAR

In 1963 at Army, Dietzel invented the Roger Staubach drill to contain Navy's star quarterback. The scheme nearly worked . . . but the clock ran out and Army fell to Navy 21–15. *Photo courtesy of U.S. Military Academy Library*

THE BOYS ARE BACK IN TOWN Ara Parseghian (second from left) and Paul Dietzel (second from right) have a laugh with old Miami friends, teammate Robert Raymond, coach George Blackburn, and trainer Jay Colville. *Photo reprinted with permission of Miami University, Oxford, OH*

BO KNOWS FOOTBALL
The 1969 Michigan victory
over number one–ranked
Ohio State launched Bo
Schembechler's career.
Woody Hayes himself told
Bo later, "Bo, you'll never
win a bigger game."
*Photo courtesy of Bentley Historical
Library, University of Michigan*

CARRIED AWAY With Cozza's Yale team winning or sharing four Ivy League titles in the '70s, he couldn't bring himself to leave the job, despite offers for better ones. *Yale Athletic Dept. Archives*

HINDSIGHT'S 20–20
Looking back, Cozza wishes
he'd retired in 1994, a year
Yale defeated the University
of Connecticut and Harvard.
He hung on for two more years,
with only five wins between them.
Yale Athletic Dept. Archives

"COACH, PUT US IN" Calvin Hill and teammate Brian Dowling asked Yale coach Carm Cozza, in the waning moments of the 1968 Yale-Harvard Game, just as Harvard was threatening to tie the score up, to let them go in on defense. Cozza refused. Harvard "won" 28–28. *Yale Athletic Dept. Archives*

"BD" As a student at Yale, Garry Trudeau created a character named "BD" for his comic strip "Bull Tales" (later to become "Doonesbury") in the *Yale Daily News* based on Yale quarterback phenomenon Brian Dowling. Dowling created the kind of magic that caused students at Yale to hang signs around campus that read: GOD WEARS NO. 10. *Yale Athletic Dept. Archives*

DOWN AND OUT IN INDIANA
During Bill Mallory's years at
Indiana, expectations were so low
that he was named Big Ten Coach
of the Year in 1986 for guiding his
team to a 6-6 season. *Indiana University
Archives (#87-655-19)*

ONE SCRAPPY KID Though Indiana fans at a basketball game
in the Hoosier Dome in 1987 booed when they heard Anthony
Thompson finished second in the Heisman Trophy race, Bill
Mallory couldn't be disappointed. He retired Thompson's number
32 jersey at the end-of-the-year banquet. *Indiana University Archives*

ALMOST HEAVEN
Don Nehlen created
the flying "WV" symbol
for the West Virginia
helmets, opened his
first season in a new
Mountaineer Field in
front of a crowd that
included John Denver,
and gave the state a
new-found appetite
for victory. *Photo courtesy*
of West Virginia University
Athletic Archives

BEYOND HEAVEN After the success of the 1988 season, the job
offers came pouring in for Don Nehlen, but he chose to stay in
West Virginia. Charleston *(W.Va.)* Daily Mail

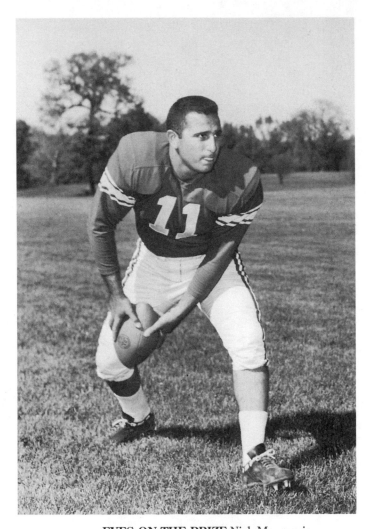

EYES ON THE PRIZE Nick Mourouzis,
John Pont's star quarterback at Miami,
might have gone on to high-profile
coaching, but found a happy home at
Division III DePauw University.
*Photo reprinted with permission of Miami University,
Oxford, OH*

PART II

Twilight

10

Moves

In 1984, Sid Gillman was in Los Angeles, working with Steve Young on his moves. Young, who was just beginning his pro career for the USFL L.A. Express, began to complain that it was getting too dark to see. Gillman barked back, "I don't care, we got to get this straight."

When darkness fell dramatically enough to impress even Gillman, the two watched film together until Gillman fell asleep. Young drove his coach home.

That short-lived partnership marked the beginning of one career and the closure of the other. Where Young went and how Gillman got there are equally impressive.

Gillman first moved from Ohio to the West Coast in 1955 to enter the ranks of pro coaches: for the Los Angeles Rams. He was Dorothy—as he would find—no longer in Kansas...or in Gillman's case, Ohio. He would, over time, learn that there was "no place like home." To survive in the football wilds outside Ohio, Gillman would develop and maintain the role of the "man behind the curtain."

While with the Rams, he started the first film exchange in the NFL. He was, moreover, studying what his own players could do, particularly Tom Fears. "The main thing was Fears," he said. "We were just beginning to understand how moves are made by a receiver. Fears was one of the greatest 'move' men in the history of the game. He didn't have much speed, but he could turn 'em on their heads. We studied Fears and we began to coach what he was doing."

If Gillman expected to find an easy coaching situation with Fears and quarterback Norm Van Brocklin, he was naive. Van Brocklin referred to Sid Gillman as "the rabbi." "I wanted to coach the team," said Van Brocklin, "and Gillman wouldn't let me."

The Rams won their conference, then lost in the championship game to Otto Graham's Browns. In the locker room after the loss, spirits were still high. Tex Schramm, the general manager, warned Gillman, "Just remember it isn't always going to be this easy."

His words were prophetic. Gillman's Rams floundered through the following seasons with records of 4–8, 6–6, 8–4, and 2–10. To avoid the impending ax, he submitted his resignation.

At that point in 1959, Gillman pondered a move out of the world of football—not back to Kansas—but to that which encompasses everything else: Wall Street.

Before embarking on his hejira east, he received a phone call from the other side of town. It was former Notre Dame coach Frank Leahy, who had been appointed general manager of the Los Angeles Chargers, a team just created to compete in the newly conceived AFL. Gillman gladly accepted Leahy's invitation to join the Chargers' franchise as head coach.

That job was the inverse of Wall Street; the fledgling league had no clout, no image, no television contracts, no money, no big-name players.

Gillman once even took his Chargers to Rough Acres Ranch for preseason training. The dirt fields and spare barracks were Bear Bryant–style in their potential cruelty, but really the team was just there to save a buck.

With the Chargers, Gillman was really slumming it. He didn't seem to mind, though. In fact, it offered him the greatest stimulation. Beneath the fragility of the 1959 AFL in general and the Chargers in particular were pristine muscles and nerves for Gillman to transform.

Above all, Gillman sought to build another home for his brain.

Gillman might have chosen Jack Kemp, the quarterback who drove the relocated San Diego Chargers to two consecutive AFL West titles in 1960 and 1961. Kemp was certainly smart enough. But during the 1962 season, Kemp shattered his finger on a defender's helmet. When Gillman waived his quarterback from the next game, Kemp's name appeared on a waiver wire, a precarious place to be because of one obscure rule: a player waived a week before a weekend game could not be reclaimed by his team till the following week. Gillman, assuming that no one would pursue the implementation of such a strange rule, expected to be able to pick up Kemp again without any problem.

An inside tip about both the rule and Kemp's status found its way to the ears of Buffalo Bills' owner Ralph Wilson. He leaped through the loophole, snatching up Kemp for a mere hundred dollars.

As this was the advent of the AFL, years before the era of lawyers and their excessive but essential articulations of right and wrong, Kemp slipped away from San Diego. Over time, Kemp lived out what might have been Gillman's worst nightmare at that time. The 1964 Buffalo team he led ousted the Chargers from the apex of the AFL and replicated that success the following year. Kemp earned all-pro status four times, and was AFL MVP in 1965.

No matter. Quarterbacks John Hadl and Tobin Rote, particularly in tandem with receiver Lance Alworth, supplied the offensive fire Gillman wanted.

From a distance and up close, Lance Alworth looked like Adam before the fall: long, lithe legs and arms, a baby face, pale crew cut, and a stride so light and natural that he seemed to be more animal than man. Though some compared him to a horse and others to a deer, the latter led to the nickname that stuck: Bambi. He was, if not Gillman's brain, his pet. "If Lance had played the piano," said Gillman in a sentimental mood, "he would have probably sounded like Arthur Rubenstein."

Hadl could throw the long passes as well as the short passes, and Alworth could leap for all of them. Some wondered if he had eyes in the back of his head.

Nevertheless, while coaching at Miami, Gillman realized that the Solomon on the field didn't have to play quarterback. Regardless of position, the brain on his team had to control the beginning, middle, and end of a play. In light of the complex, shifting, and unpredictable pass attacks Gillman was developing, only a man of great patience could act as judge, jury, and executioner all at once.

Ron Mix, a gentle giant, an offensive tackle, young, drafted to the Chargers straight from USC in 1959, possessed all the ability to be judge, jury, and executioner. His line coach accurately dubbed him the "Intellectual Assassin"; he monitored the line of scrimmage as if he were a guard atop the Berlin Wall.

Mix's ability to hold the line offered sound protection and plenty of decision-making time for quarterback John Hadl. With that portion of a play accounted for, Gillman began to fiddle with the other side—the receivers, running backs, and tight ends. He figured that if he could precisely choreograph the play on one side of the line of scrimmage, he could do it on the other.

Gillman soon concocted a passing offense unlike any seen before. He added tight ends and running backs into his intricate patterns as receivers, so that five pass-eligible players spread up the field, forcing the defense to cover a greater expanse of territory.

"Sid's system was as complex as any in history," said Bill Walsh. "He had a term for every pass pattern for every receiver. It took years for some people to learn."

His system—which came to be known as the West Coast Offense—moved where he couldn't. Walsh learned Gillman's system in Oakland from Gillman's former assistant, Al Davis. In 1979, Walsh carried it to the San Francisco 49ers, and the good word still continues to spread throughout the NFL and college ranks.

Inspired by Mix, Hadl, Rote, and Alworth's ability, Gillman applied this new kind of offense most successfully in 1963. Though it seemed to Alworth that "the quarterback did all the reading, all the work," without Mix managing the timing and Alworth snatching passes from thin air, the West Coast Offense would never have reached fruition.

When Paul Dietzel visited his mentor during these years, he sat in on the Charger coaches' "chalk talk." Dietzel had no idea what Gillman was talking about.

The 1963 season was a magical one. The team scored 399 points, and although Alworth was responsible for just eleven touchdowns, the passing attack utilized nine different receivers, most notably tight ends Dave Kocourek and Jacques MacKinnon, each of whom averaged more than sixteen yards a reception.

Despite Gillman's radical concepts, he maintained a conservative demeanor. Generally, he wore a bow tie and sport coat at the outset of a game, tossing the jacket when the action heated up. On the sidelines, he had a Wall Street air about him. Then, there was a third side to him: he was as tough, excessive, and stunningly gentle as the Godfather. After his 1963 squad defeated the Boston Patriots 51–10 in the AFL championship, Gillman footed the bill for a night's worth of partying in which his entire team engaged.

Why not celebrate? Even though the system had not yet constructed an AFL vs. NFL Super Bowl, George Halas, coach of the 1963 NFL champion Chicago Bears, admitted that the Chargers would have won such a confrontation. Simply, Gillman's team was the best in the country.

But the next two seasons were shadows of the ideal of '63. In both '64 and '65 they fell in the league championship to the Buffalo Bills, with Kemp at quarterback. Then the Chargers came under new ownership in 1966. Other things were changing, too. In the mid-sixties, along with the increased emphasis on weight training—supervised for the Chargers by former Baton Rouge gym owner Alvin Roy—came less virtuous supplements. Roy, who had trained Paul Dietzel's LSU running back Billy Cannon, told the athletes that he had picked up tips from the "Rooskies" about a drug called Dianabol. Though he explained that the pills would simply aid in the assimilation of protein, they were actually steroids.

Dianabol was still in use among San Diego players, Ron Mix later reported, when he left the team in 1969.

At the close of the 1969 season, Gillman, too, resigned from his post with the Chargers, because of chronic ulcers. For a year his body said, "No," but his mind, after a year, drowned out the sound with a word: "Move."

The odyssey began. In 1971, he gave San Diego one more season, but a compulsion to move carried him elsewhere the following season. It drove him to Dallas in 1972, where he assisted Tom Landry, then the next year to Houston to be general manager of the Oilers. Midway through the season he fired head coach Bill Peterson, and Gillman returned to the sidelines to finish out that season and to coach the next, earning the AFL coach-of-the-year honors for turning a 1–13 team around to a 7–7 record in 1974.

The odyssey continued. Along the way, Gillman's role rarefied: he ceased to be a head coach, devoting himself solely to the shaping of an offense. In 1977, he acted as offensive coordinator for the Chicago Bears. In 1979, he joined up with Dick Vermeil and the Philadelphia Eagles. At their first meeting, Vermeil was so grateful to have Gillman there, he broke down in tears. Vermeil handed the quarterbacks—among them Ron Jaworski—over to Gillman. In 1980, the Eagles reached the Super Bowl. In 1983, he went to the USFL L.A. Express, and, though that league folded after only a few seasons, under its auspices Gillman made yet another lasting contribution to football lore: Steve Young. He returned to the Eagles in 1985 to coach the quarterbacks. Then in 1987, he pitched in to guide the University of Pittsburgh team under coach Mike Gottfried to an 8–4 season.

Though he has been retired since the 1987 season, he still studies film, keeping up to date on the game and its players. Joe Theismann, quarterback first for Ara Parseghian's Notre Dame team, then for the Washington Redskins, remarked on football in the last decade, "You used to have half a dozen or so exceptional quarterbacks. Unitas, Bradshaw, Starr, Hadl, Jurgensen, Namath. If they played well, the team won. Today the primary job of a quarterback is not to win games, it's to make the right decisions and not lose them." Gillman would not be so cynical; he's a great admirer of John Elway, Randall Cunningham, and Troy Aikman. On those coming up the ranks he reserves judgment, but he's never shy with praise. He enjoys the year-to-year changes of personality and style.

In Gillman's backyard in La Costa, California, is a pool the shape of a football. It's subtle—just an oval that comes to a point on the two narrow ends. It suits the scene perfectly as it seems to suggest, "Come, jump into me."

But I can't imagine Gillman backstroking through sun-warmed water. He's just too busy watching film.

I foolishly visited him in his home on a Saturday afternoon in October. During our chat, a television in the next room, tuned to a football game, offered a fitting soundtrack. The Doppler cheers, the strains of marching bands, and the apoplectic announcers, muted by one wall, sounded like a hybrid of Cole Porter and the Attica prison riot. Though I had no idea what game was progressing nor what other games going on simultaneously might easily be accessed with the flick of a remote, I felt guilty for keeping him away from the nearest font of football.

Then I suspected I wasn't. I firmly believe I saw him, several times, lose all consciousness of my presence, using a sixth sense only football coaches possess to not only hear the sounds of the game emitted from the far-off TV, but to actually see the game itself, from all angles, better than fans huddled on splintered seats in the actual stadium, better than the gum-chewing coaches on the actual sideline. I know I have seen my father sucked away from a conversation via the extrasensory vacuum that flicks on immediately in the proximity of anything football related. Gillman, I imagine, must be so susceptible to that phenomenon that a sizable sepia-toned picture of a game develops from one tiny stimulus, one primal sound: *I, T, wing T, wishbone . . .*

Later, at his leisure, playing back the reels of his imagination, rewinding at certain points, he nods with pleasure at what each team executed properly, scrutinizes carefully what each bungled, and then arrives at appropriate solutions.

Why is there so much trouble these days in converting the ideal into the real?

Maybe Esther Gillman knows. The Gillmans' children, Lyle, Bobby, Terry, and Tom, came of age in two different eras. Lyle and Bobby sprang from the early sixties, when life for most of America was a black-and-white movie still. Terry and Tom, though, shot up from the late sixties, a Charybdis of psychedelia. When Sid's wife Esther discussed her offspring with me, she divided them into those pairs, adopting an entirely different tone to depict each. On the subject of Lyle and Bobby, her voice spun like a scratchy Louis Prima record. They attended college in Ohio and embraced Ohio values. After Friday night dates, they would go to their parents' bedroom to check in and to share all the details of the evening. Esther describing them was Donna Reed, sweet, secure, black and white.

Moving on to the subject of Tom and Terry, her voice becomes amused and somewhat naughty. In contrast to their older siblings, she reports, the younger two pilgrimaged to the mecca of the rebellious sixties: the University of California at Berkeley. "They're the liberal thinkers," she says, giving a sardonic emphasis to the word "liberal." That Terry, now a Peace Corps worker in South Africa, and Tom, who never played football, are so clearly the antithesis of Lyle and Bobby thrills Esther not because the former are better than the latter but because the contrast kept motherhood stimulating for her. "Tom and Terry taught me a lot," says Esther. She seems grateful to have learned the lessons of two separate worlds.

In the sixties and seventies the attitudes toward race, gender, war, government, and individual responsibility changed so rapidly that some were exhilarated, some frightened, some simply left behind. Gillman's children, as they grew up, were right on pace. Their father, at times, caught up, then lost a lot of ground. But in Gillman's desire to continue changing, he was able to keep himself on a lofty level.

When Sid Gillman moved from college football to the pros, he left the sweet security of Ohio for something much riskier and more stimulating. But risk and stimulation, with time, could sour. Moving, it would turn out, kept the ideal of football in front of him and the ugly reality behind him.

This is my fantasy, of course. I have no idea, really, how the mind of a football genius operates. All I know is that if the high school at which I teach had a football team, I would give Sid Gillman my life savings (a gesture, in actuality, more symbolic than lucrative) to make a final move and coach us for just one ideal season. My home in Bethlehem, Pennsylvania, is not quite Ohio, but all Gillman ever really needs to feel at home are the *X*s and *O*s of pure football.

11

Irony

Woody Hayes's Ohio State team earned the Big Ten berth in the Rose Bowl each season from 1972 to 1975. From the outset of his "Ten-Year War" with Bo Schembechler, the two programs put such a lock on the Rose Bowl slot that Big Ten commissioners were forced to reevaluate their position that other league teams could not accept bids from other bowls. Until 1974, Big Ten commissioners upheld this isolationist policy, and coaches followed suit: they played their schedules of league and other traditional and/or local rivals monomaniacally, as if west of Iowa, east of Columbus, and south of Bloomington there festered a type of football lacking in any sepia-toned splendor.

But finally, in 1975, when the Ohio State team led by two-time Heisman winner Archie Griffin maintained its lock on the Rose Bowl, several Big Ten bridesmaids for the first time found themselves playing postseason games in settings other than Pasadena.

What no one could guess at that time was that Hayes's success would prove to be the cause of his downfall.

How could anyone? Everything seemed so perfect. Throughout the early seventies, the philosophy that Hayes preached— of commitment, honesty, and stoicism—was abundantly evident in every aspect of the program. He kept the program lean—in 1972, for example, there were only sixteen scholarship athletes despite the accepted ceiling of thirty. He fined linebacker Ken Kuhn for leaving training camp... because he drove six hundred miles to Connecticut to pursuade fellow linebacker Lou Pietrini to return to the team. As far as Hayes was concerned, that Kuhn had done the right thing was less important than the fact that he had broken the rules.

It was tough love, but tinged with a selflessness that made Hayes his players' second father. They respected his toughness. He was as demanding of himself as he was of others. He wore short-sleeved shirts in even the coldest of weather, only conceding to the concern for frostbite by layering a second or a third short-sleeved shirt on top of the first. Hayes spoke all over the country, seldom accepting any honorarium for his efforts. Once, on his way to make a speech at the Canton Gridiron Club, a snowstorm came up, his car got stuck, and he walked for hours to reach his final destination. He walked in at 10:15, hours late, ready to talk.

His idiosyncrasies and feistiness were, unarguably, paying

off. He could turn in Michigan State for NCAA violations, turn away Jack Nicklaus from the game of football, and every choice to all eyes was absolutely correct.

Especially in Archie Griffin, one of those sixteen scholarship athletes, everything that he did on the field, all the ideals of Hayes's coaching were the most refined. Griffin was the poster child for "three yards and a cloud of dust." He seemed disinterested in self-promotion, only in absorbing the coaching of Woody Hayes.

Though, in 1973, Griffin took his team to its annual matchup with Michigan undefeated, even he couldn't rise above the emotions of that contest. The game ended in a frustrating 10–10 stalemate. Afterward, Michigan, by all rights, deserved to go to the Rose Bowl. Big Ten commissioners, though, felt Ohio State would represent the conference better in the matchup against USC. Really, they were electing to match Archie Griffin against his USC running back counterpart Anthony Davis.

For the first half of that Rose Bowl, this deliberate matchup was a moot point in the game. USC was first to put points on the board with kicker Chris Limahelu's forty-seven-yard field goal. Then Ohio State missed its own field goal attempt, but capitalized on a USC offsides penalty, which allowed fullback Pete Johnson the opportunity for six points of his own.

Limahelu launched another successful field goal; Davis found a new role in passing to tight end Jake McKay for a touchdown. Though a two-point conversion gave USC a 14–7 edge, Johnson thundered in another touchdown to even up the score.

Davis finally shoved through the line from the one-yard line for his own touchdown, but Ohio State swiftly responded with an unprecedentedly long, thirty-nine-yard pass from quarterback Corny Greene to tight end Fred Pugac, which led to a third Johnson touchdown. Less than a minute later, Greene faked a pass, then juked off tackle to score, putting Ohio State up 28–21.

Where was Griffin? Waiting his turn. He set up the next touchdown with a twenty-five-yard run, then scored the final touchdown of the game with a forty-seven-yard run. With that, Ohio State put the last nail in the 42–21 coffin.

Apparently, Griffin could do everything right, including share the glory.

The following year, the burden of the Rose Bowl game rested almost entirely on Griffin's shoulders. Though he again did everything right, he could not win that game alone. Hayes had never taught him how to do that. It wasn't a part of the philosophy.

Irony is an often misused word with a very specific meaning: it is the occurrence of the exact opposite of that which is expected. In light of the wild successes Hayes and his compatriot Bo Schembechler experienced in the early seventies, one could only have anticipated further glory. But the exact opposite occurred.

After Griffin graduated, Hayes seemed to age. He began to sport long sleeves in cold weather. His teams, every once in a while, lost. In 1976, after a 22–0 thrashing by Michigan, Ohio State formally relinquished its domination of the "Ten-Year War." A Woody Hayes team would never again play in the Rose Bowl.

No matter; precisely because of early dominance in Rose Bowl appearances, Ohio State could go to postseason games other than the Rose Bowl. In 1976, they lost to Colorado in the Orange Bowl 27–10; in 1977, they lost to Alabama 35–6 in the Sugar Bowl. Then, in 1978, they found themselves, despite a 7–3–1 record and a fourth-place standing in the Big Ten, scheduled to play Clemson in the Gator Bowl.

The Columbus newspapers were less generous than the Gator Bowl selection committee. The sportswriters were ruthless in their criticism of Hayes, particularly in his choice, week in and week out, to start freshman quarterback Art Schlichter, whose dependability was widely questioned. But Hayes remained loyal to the young player. Despite outcry after outcry, he put Schlichter at the helm of the offense in the Gator Bowl game, from beginning to end.

I remember the game for a few reasons. Despite the countless football games I attended while growing up, I sat with my father to watch games on television only in the minute window of time he was home instead of coaching. Because the Ivy League forbade its members to accept invitations to bowl games, late December and New Year's Day found my father at home in an armchair, while I sat on the couch, nibbling snacks. He was quiet during games—no commentary, no criticism—perfectly content watching someone else coach. It was a safe mirror: he was not responsible for whatever blemish he saw.

In 1978 we watched that Gator Bowl together. It was a night game, and though I didn't much care about the game itself, I was content to let it slowly lull me to sleep. I didn't know much about the teams; the treat, really, was watching with my father.

Late in the game, I opened my eyes to see that the score was close, Clemson up 17–15, with Ohio State driving. I sat up. My father looked as he did before I nodded off, calmly watching, pleased he was in his chair and not on the field.

Schlichter sent up a pass, which was handily intercepted by Clemson's Charlie Bauman. Bauman went down near the Ohio State bench. As he stood, Hayes ran over, swinging his arms in characteristically exuberant arcs. One swing came up and jammed into Bauman's neck, just below his facemask. Hayes looked like a father protecting his son from the neigh-borhood bully.

I had seen my father cry on only one other occasion, when his father died. It was morning, and I sped into the kitchen to munch a piece of toast before leaving for the bus stop. I pulled up short when I saw my father kneeling before the fireplace, poking sparks, hiding his face.

My father wielded no power to alter the course of events leading to the end of my grandfather's life or of Woody Hayes's career. I suspect that, if he had possessed such ability he would have used it then, no matter how dire the consequences, if only to assuage his own feelings of helplessness.

The many years and then the final season leading up to that moment were haunted by foreshadowings of the final tragedy, but not, I believe, by the specific demons to which other writers point. Many have chronicled the litany of Hayes's public explosions throughout his career at Ohio State, suggesting that the Gator Bowl fiasco was inevitable. The lists are so lengthy and the performances Hayes gave are so outrageous that I could acknowledge a pattern but for one variable: he hit an athlete. That wasn't like him. To help athletes was his primary goal, so he only hit—metaphorically or literally—those who he felt sabotaged his mission.

Hayes embodied masculinity in every way: athlete, husband, father, general, sage. In all his roles, he upheld physical, intellectual, and moral strength. He consistently purged the frailty from the minds and bodies of his athletes and wouldn't give the time of day to any weakness in himself.

As a result, he could neither expose nor even fully accept that he was ill. That was his greatest weakness, and he paid for it.

Within Hayes's thick bark lurked type 2 diabetes—with which he was diagnosed at the age of fifty in 1963—perhaps the most subtle and misunderstood disease. If unmanaged for several years, it can foster blindness, paraplegia, death. If ignored for only a day, it can decimate consciousness so completely that action is independent of mind, memory, and even morals.

On more than one occasion, Bo Schembechler has pointed to Hayes's diabetes. Bo reported that Hayes sometimes failed to follow the prescribed regimen for type 2 diabetes. Specifically, Hayes did not always take the prescribed oral medication he was supposed to: sulfonylureas, a drug designed to encourage the pancreas to produce more insulin. However, even if he were faithful in taking his medication, it had a pronounced side effect: it often caused hypoglycemia, particularly in those with erratic eating habits.

That fact, accompanied by an understanding of Hayes's lifestyle, which couldn't possibly allow for the dietary and other personal regulations diabetes demands, confirms Schembechler's conclusion: Hayes's blood sugar was "out of whack." Deep in a hypoglycemic haze, a crippled version of Hayes slugged that player without even knowing he did it.

Bo Schembechler rushed to set up a meeting with his friend. He found a midway point between Columbus and Ann Arbor, the Bowling Green house of their old colleague Doyt Perry. When Schembechler first broached the topic of the event, Hayes had no recollection of hitting the Clemson player. Only after watching the film would he fully accept what had happened.

Because pointing to an illness could be perceived as making excuses, at least in 1978, Hayes accepted the university's decision to usher out the old man. That stoicism fits Hayes's character. Moreover, with his endless days, incessant traveling, unpredictable mealtimes, spontaneous nocturnal forays to rush to the aid of athletes, colleagues, former athletes... he scarcely sustained the moderate lifestyle that diabetes demands.

To this day, Ohio State's Web site writes off Hayes's behavior in the Gator Bowl as a "temper tantrum." It's still not okay to admit being sick. It still seems to be regarded not as a viable explanation, but as a cheap way out.

Despite his prominence in not only Ohio but also the rest of the country, Woody Hayes kept his home number listed in the local phone book. To have an unlisted number would have, no doubt, struck Hayes as a pretension. He wasn't one to pretend he was someone he was not.

That Hayes kept his diabetes to himself, though, is not an inconsistency, because his toughness had, for so long, canceled out his illness. It is, however, an irony that his only secret is the thing that, in the end, left him most exposed.

When greatness collapses and irony prevails, a true hero endures. Though Hayes was completely transformed in the public's view, he didn't die at that moment, or even change; he refused to. He remained in Columbus, he spoke in public, he promoted his former players. In some ways, his life did not skip a beat.

Throughout his career, he was never one to hide. Somehow he knew that if he endeavored to close off communication with the world, some sneaky armchair coach would have found him out and passed address, number, make of car, and financial information around, so Hayes would have, at the very least, gotten plenty of calls in the middle of the night from naysayers. So he kept the lines open. Sometimes he invited late-night callers to come on over for an early breakfast.

Fundamentally, he liked everybody. His combined confidence in himself and interest in others engendered Hayes's inclusion of friends, enemies, strangers. Though success granted him the right to isolate himself, he never saw it that way. Rather, success widened the passage in which he encountered more people.

When Hayes first visited the Schembechlers' Ann Arbor home, he was most attentive to Millie, addressing her as "Mrs. Schembechler" in a tone of humble deference. Young Shemy Schembechler couldn't believe it. He always assumed he would despise his father's rival. Meeting the man, he found nothing to despise.

Because he needed to be connected, Hayes couldn't stand to vacation, feeling, while he was gone, that everything he had built at Ohio State crumbled instantly into rubble. Once, while mountain climbing in the Alps with a group of Ohio State alumni, he learned that a player wasn't making the grades needed to maintain eligibility. He flew straight home.

But he had one retreat from football, a tiny two-room cabin set in the hills of southeast Ohio. It called to mind Thoreau, Emerson, and the other American idealists he so admired. Though he seldom had time to retreat to this hermitage, when he did he was completely removed from the furor of football and suspended in a timeless American dream.

In 1998, that cabin fell prey to another Americanism: money. It was sold at an Ohio State alumni auction for nearly $100,000 to a person who "wanted to feel the...presence of a legend."

Hayes, I suspect, would have been embarrassed that the place went for so much. If his ghost still rambles through those rooms and the surrounding buckeye trees, he is musing on the purity of nature, of human endeavors, and of football. Because he could not be bought or sold, I cannot imagine he would want that fate to befall his possessions. In a heartbeat, he'd give that cabin away and find another Ohio hillside to haunt.

12

Knowing

After the 1968 Yale-Harvard game, the Harvard student newspaper, the *Harvard Crimson,* announced: "Harvard beats Yale, 29–29." That headline identified one of the occasions in football history in which a tie was considered a victory. The Yale community felt the inverse, regarding the game as a biting loss.

Ties are many things. Sometimes, they are a Pyrrhic victory in what had been thought an impossible situation. To spectators, they are a wild ride that leaves the stomach churning. Most of the time, though, they are like germs, something to avoid. They suggest the kind of carelessness and apathy that causes people to go out in the cold with wet hair.

Early on, Ara Parseghian learned that ties can be regarded as noxious. In 1946, the Miami team on which he played found themselves behind 17–20 to Miami of Florida. Nearing the end of the game, Miami was in reach of a field goal on fourth down. It was a safe way to tie the game.

Coach Sid Gillman, though, chose to go for the touchdown. The attempt, unfortunately, was stopped short. Nevertheless, Gillman and his staff felt they had done the right thing: gambling for a win was gutsier, more heroic than settling for a tie.

But Notre Dame's history offered Parseghian conflicting evidence about ties.

The 1946 Army–Notre Dame clash was an example of a satisfying tie. In the 1944 and 1945 confrontations with Colonel Blaik's Army team, Notre Dame lost by a combined score of 107–0. Those years, Army had earned national championships; they were expected to do the same in 1946. However, on a November afternoon in Yankee Stadium, Notre Dame stopped Army's pair of running backs, Heisman winner Glenn Davis and his cohort Doc Blanchard—known as Mr. Outside and Mr. Inside—and tightly maneuvered the game to an 0–0 tie. The students at Notre Dame were so ecstatic about their shutdown of the number one team that they formed a society called SPATNC: the Society for the Prevention of Army's Third National Championship. This society deluged Colonel Blaik with a seemingly unending stream of hostile, denigrating letters. And at the end of the season, Notre Dame was ranked number one, while Army finished number two.

Although this tie worked to Notre Dame's benefit, for

Colonel Blaik the tie with Notre Dame had the effect of a defeat. Generally, under most circumstances, tying is synonymous with losing for at least one party. Oddly enough, however, the Army-Navy tie of 1926 proved to be a loss for neither the Army nor the Navy coach.

On November 27, 1926, in Soldier Field in Chicago, Biff Jones anticipated Paul Dietzel by using clever substitution of his second-string Army squad to combat a 14–0 deficit to Navy. By the third quarter, with the first string fresh from rest, Army charged past Navy 21–14.

In the last five minutes of the game, Navy intercepted an Army pass, hitting the extra point to tie the score. Among the 110,000 fans witnessing this heated contest was Notre Dame coach Knute Rockne, whose team, without their coach, was battling Carnegie Tech, a team Rockne was confident his athletes could handle. To his surprise, the underdog Carnegie Tech defeated Notre Dame 19–0, a loss that mushroomed into a greater disappointment. Though Rockne's team had defeated Army earlier in the season, Army was awarded the 1926 national championship, and Notre Dame took second behind them.

Parseghian knew ties; Notre Dame knew ties. But neither knew the full extent of their drama until Parseghian played his own role in Notre Dame's epic of ties.

The role he assumed in that tale, early on, was that of a hero, the heir to Rockne, whose record at Notre Dame from

1918 to 1930 was 105–12–5, and to Frank Leahy, Rockne's spunky protégé, whose record was 87–11–9 from 1941 to 1943 and 1946 to 1953. Parseghian achieved status equal to these legends in two years, with a near-perfect 1964 season, a respectable 7–2–1 record in 1965, and a charisma that had won the hearts of the local and national Notre Dame following.

As a result, Parseghian entered the 1966 season with the utmost confidence.

He maintained it, week after week. Notre Dame marched through victory after victory, Saturday after Saturday, shutting out Army, North Carolina, Oklahoma, Pittsburgh, and Duke. In eight straight games only Purdue, Northwestern, and Navy scored at all—and a mere 28 points at that—while Notre Dame amassed 301 points against its opponents.

Then, during the days before November 19, a bitter wind blew into Indiana from Michigan, and the mood at Notre Dame sobered. Parseghian's undefeated team, ranked number one in the nation, was about to take on the undefeated number two team, Michigan State.

The mood darkened further when, the day before the game, star running back Nick Eddy injured his shoulder in East Lansing getting off the train.

After the kickoff, Notre Dame took another hit, then another. In the first quarter, quarterback Terry Hanratty was removed from the game one play after a devastating tackle from Michigan State's defensive lineman Bubba Smith. On the next play, Notre Dame's Kevin Hardy attempted a punt, but the snap was so low that he was forced to scramble for the ball. When he gained control of it, he had no time to kick. Instead, he heaved the ball in the air. It flew toward center George Goeddeke, who had no idea that Hardy had done anything but punt. Michigan State defenseman Jess Phillips thought Goeddeke knew. He slammed into Goeddeke's knee with his helmet, and Notre Dame lost their All-American center.

With 1:40 gone in the second quarter, Michigan State's fullback, Regis Cavender, ignoring pain caused by a rib injury and a strained ligament in his left shoulder, led an aggressive drive down the field. Notre Dame's defense seemed helpless. From the four-yard line, Cavender ran for a touchdown.

An offsides penalty on Notre Dame in the next set of plays deprived them of a first down. Michigan State took possession of the ball again on their own nineteen-yard line. On second and ten, Michigan State quarterback Jimmy Raye ran for thirty yards. Two plays later, he put up a pass that was intercepted by Jim Lynch; Lynch ran with it, took a hit, and dropped the ball. Michigan State recovered and drove for a field goal.

Later in the second quarter, despite its depleted ranks, the Notre Dame offense pulled together. Second-string quarterback Coley O'Brien, on second and thirty-four, scrambled to find running back Bob Gladieux for a touchdown. The teams went into the locker room with a close score: 10–7.

From the outset of the third quarter, both teams bungled. Michigan State fumbled the opening kickoff; on the next play, a long O'Brien pass to Rocky Bleier, Michigan State intercepted. The two teams punted back and forth. Adding to the frustration, Notre Dame's Bob Gladieux was forced to leave the game because of a bruised thigh.

But at the end of the third quarter, third-string running back Dave Haley helped Notre Dame launch an aggressive drive. O'Brien hit Haley for a twenty-three-yard pass on the first play, taking him to the Michigan State thirty-yard line. Larry Conjar gained five yards; Haley chewed up four and then four again; Bleier for five; Conjar for two; O'Brien moved to pass, danced past Bubba Smith, and was sacked at the line of scrimmage.

A few seconds into the fourth quarter, Joe Azzaro scored three points with an eighteen-yard field goal, tying the score 10–10.

Michigan State proceeded to concentrate on passing, but Notre Dame's defense was wise to it. Shut down, Michigan State was forced to punt.

On the next set of plays, O'Brien had lost the cool that had facilitated the previous field goal. After he threw a pass well over a receiver's head, Notre Dame punted.

O'Brien's passes had become so wild that Parseghian pulled him aside. Knowing O'Brien was diabetic, he worried that O'Brien's blood level was askew. O'Brien assured his coach he could play.

He went back in sooner than expected. Notre Dame safety Tom Schoen executed a brilliant interception at the Michigan State forty-nine-yard line and took off for the end zone. A

Michigan State player desperately reached for Schoen's jersey, bringing him down at the eighteen. Conjar picked up two yards. Parseghian, to trip up Michigan State, sent in a new blocking scheme. It didn't go as planned, and Haley lost eight yards. On third down, O'Brien threw up a pass. It was blocked.

Azzaro, the man who had kicked the field goal that tied the game for Notre Dame, ran in to earn the victory. The snap and the placement were flawless. Azzaro stepped to the ball smoothly. The ball lofted straight toward the goalposts.

Then it floated to the right, a foot and a half wide of the goalpost.

Michigan State ate up two minutes of the clock before they had no choice but to punt. Notre Dame ran it down on their own thirty-yard line with 1:24 remaining.

Deep in their own territory, Parseghian knew any mistake would be costly. So he kept the ball on the ground: O'Brien around the end for four; Bleier on a draw for three; a handoff to Conjar for two; a big push on fourth down for two more yards and first down.

The crowd booed; the Michigan State defense taunted. Even the Notre Dame players wondered: why didn't Parseghian call a pass?

Finally, with ten seconds left in the game, he did. Bubba Smith hit O'Brien for a loss of seven yards as the clock ran out.

After the game, Parseghian offered two explanations for his caution in the final plays of the game; the first: the Notre

Dame second-string quarterback, Coley O'Brien, was a diabetic, and his blood sugar levels were so skewed that he was having trouble throwing the ball; the second: Parseghian didn't want his team to make a mistake that could lead to a Michigan State score. A loss would eliminate any chance for the national championship.

Even though Notre Dame's defeat of USC the following week by 51–0 secured the national championship for Parseghian and his team, he came under merciless scrutiny and criticism. The media dubbed him "chicken," "rabbit," "mouse." They egged on Bubba Smith to bad-mouth Parseghian. Everything Notre Dame had accomplished that season was moot because of the microscope the world had focused on one tie game.

For a long time after that game, Parseghian chewed on the painful lesson that winning, to the most vocal, the most powerful, is everything.

He learned other things, too. He discovered the bitterness of football success: "In coaching," he said, "the best you can do is win them all. Go to a bowl game and win the bowl game. But the next year the best you can do is only duplicate that. You can't improve on that, and the odds are way against you."

These realizations might have changed a man weaker than Parseghian. But he never lost his ability to empathize with the players, even when he was compelled to be the coach on high.

In 1967, Notre Dame did not duplicate their previous year's national championship, but went 8–2. For those two losses,

Parseghian was once again the recipient of heavy criticism. He added an addendum to his definition of coaching's bitterness: "You become a victim of your own success."

Because Parseghian is not the type to be victimized, he tapped all his intensity to generate consistent success. Only once after his 1966 championship did his team rank lower than tenth in the nation at the end of the season: in 1971 they were thirteenth. When, during the 1969 season, the university finally allowed the team to accept bowl bids, they battled Texas in the Cotton Bowl, losing in the last minutes 21–17. The following year, same setting, same opponent, Notre Dame won 24–11. Parseghian hated to lose two times in a row. In the regular season, he never did.

After the 1966 season, Parseghian learned something outside of football that did change him: his daughter Karan was diagnosed as having multiple sclerosis, a disease that also afflicted Parseghian's sister. With new eyes he turned his gaze on his family, seeing that his wife and children were far more important to him than football.

So, as his children grew up, Parseghian endeavored to give time to his family. To do so, Parseghian radically altered one common practice for coaches: recruiting. Because of Notre Dame's unique position as a national rather than a state school, potential athletes were scattered throughout every state in the country. To visit all recruits in their homes could keep him and his assistants on the road all year. So, in order to see his family and allow his staff to do the same, he did away with all personal visits. If he couldn't see all the recruits, he felt, he shouldn't see one.

Dividing time between family and football was Solomon bisecting the baby. Sunday morning was the only time he could, on a regular basis, forget his myriad football-related responsibilities and devote himself to his children. It was during those Sunday morning sessions that he transformed into the Grizzly Bear, challenging Karan, Kris, and Mike to find the elusive *secret, secret place.*

Like Bill Mallory, Parseghian would often catch the first half of his son Mike's high school football games. Once, after he had left a game midway through and reported to work, an assistant coach blurted, "Did you hear what your son did?"

Parseghian looked at him blankly.

"He just intercepted a pass. I heard it on the radio."

Though he had little time to watch his children, they devoted their time to watching him, up close or far away. His family was a part of football, not a separate entity. Katie entertained after every home game. Though she took pleasure in watching a game, she felt the pressure to win too deeply to sit demurely in the stadium. Early on in her husband's time at Notre Dame, she developed the habit of leaving a game at halftime with the excuse that she needed to prepare for her guests. Later in Parseghian's career, she ceased to go at all, preferring to watch the games on television so she could pace and mutter at will.

But Katie generally experienced great joy in her role as wife to a football coach, and generated joy for those in the football world around her. Every spring she threw a party for the players about to graduate and invited their families. Throughout the year, she helped the families of new coaches get settled in, and she held gatherings for the coaches' wives apart from their husbands, to share their common frustrations and pleasures.

Katie didn't let the frustrations wear her down. For example, the Parseghians, like the Hayeses, received phone calls day and night from irate fans. Katie learned to deliver some clever quips. On one occasion, when a nocturnal caller woke her and demanded to speak to Parseghian, she informed the caller that her husband would be happy to call him back at 5:00 A.M., when he woke up. The caller passed on the offer.

Growing up, Parseghian's children felt, for their father's sake, a responsibility to be good. When they were ready for college, they stayed close to home. Karan attended Miami for two years and then graduated from Notre Dame; Mike played football for his father while studying medicine. Kris married one of her father's players, guard Jim Humbert.

Ara Parseghian was a great father; he was a great coach. All that success, despite his best efforts, began to victimize him, as he had predicted it would. Driving Notre Dame's football machine while attending to the needs of his family took its toll on Parseghian's health. He took pills to sleep, pills for his blood pressure.

That all his accomplishments were scrutinized through the lens of Notre Dame, that he was always measured up against Rockne and Leahy, ate at him, too. Once, walking by a gilded bust of Knute Rockne in the athletic facilities, he paused and drilled his dark, penetrating stare into it.

He said to the golden image, "You started all this."

In 1974, that which Rockne started had to end, at least for Parseghian.

That year, shortly after Karan married Jim Burke, who attended seminary at Notre Dame, Parseghian knew the time had come to retire.

On Saturday mornings before Miami games, in the dawn of Parseghian's coaching when he didn't know what he didn't know, he drove the country roads around Oxford, keeping his anxiety at bay. He was possessed by a single desire: for the game to begin.

When it did, his mind became totally focused on the action, reading the other team, his own team, shaping his knowledge to fit his observations. In essence, he was solving a complex equation in which he strove to keep variables to a minimum, which required a great deal of work shown, and which had an inflexible correct answer: won.

In his eleven years at Notre Dame, everything, including football, became more complicated. Parseghian finally discovered what he didn't know and, as a result, learned many a difficult lesson.

Those lessons continued. His son Mike, a doctor practicing in Arizona, has four children, three of whom were found to have Niemann-Pick type C disease, a metabolic disorder that causes fatal damage to the nervous system. Though Parseghian knew neither his Armenian nor his French grandparents, his own grandchildren have become his purpose. From his office in South Bend, he chairs the research foundation that seeks to find a cure for this disease.

When I first met Parseghian last year in that office, I was struck by the handsomeness of his face. The parallel lines that run from the corners of his mouth down to his jaw, the shadowy cavern of pewter eyes beneath the worn leather of his forehead are the features of the aged hero, most compelling at that moment because time had transformed all his heroics into legend.

Then he moved toward me, one leg at a time, slowly, keeping his limbs straight, reaching for chairs, desks, and doorknobs as he moved, pausing after each step to regain the courage to take another. He reached for my hand.

Winning can't go on forever. The frailty of being human inevitably trips us up. When, at the end of his coaching career, human frailty gaped before Parseghian, he redefined victory. For him, it became not the singularity of being proclaimed *best, champion, number one,* of surpassing all others so that they are far behind you, shivering in their weakness. He defined it, rather, as a tie in which two disparate bodies come face-to-face, equal in their willingness to struggle and endure.

Though Parseghian's life went from football to family, family didn't win; football didn't lose. They're locked in a tie. Even now, his work devoted to family, he constantly confronts his palpable legacy.

In Parseghian's office, behind the desk, is the game ball from the 1973 Sugar Bowl game in which, on December 31, Notre Dame defeated Bear Bryant's Alabama team 24–23, earning Parseghian the Associated Press National Championship. Though he points to that game as his most memorable, his team matched that success the following year: though an 11-point underdog, Notre Dame shocked number one–ranked Alabama in the Orange Bowl on January 1, 1975, by defeating them 13–11.

Parseghian retired after that, his 234th game. Though he was only fifty years old, he was a sage in the world of football. He had come a long way from the man about whom Paul Brown remarked, "Ara doesn't know what he doesn't know." And in 1975, he knew he needed to devote himself to his family.

13

Home

John and Sandy Pont are gourmet cooks. A passion on John's part for replicating the traditional cuisine of his childhood escalated to the point that, while at Indiana, he joined a cooking club consisting of professors and Indianapolis cognoscenti that met more or less once a month in different homes. The host or hostess prepared the main dish while others supplied the other courses. Pont's specialty, logically, was paella.

A Spaniard, Pont had swarthy skin that tanned deeply from running practices and standing on the sidelines of games. His eyes were so dark a shade of brown that the pupils were indistinguishable. But by the time he reached Indiana, his hair was white and thinning. No one would have thought to call him "Spik," as he was known to his friends on the Miami football team. Even if someone had, in the late sixties such a moniker could have been neither delivered nor heard as an endearment. At best, it would have been met with silence, which is the mask over mistrust.

In his youth, issues of ethnicity seemed easy.

But then, for the world, all that changed and suddenly nothing was easy. At every university in the country in the late sixties and early seventies, the text and subtext of race relations grew volatile. Football, depending on the region, was either far ahead of or far behind the times. Miami's Boxcar Bailey, playing in the early fifties, was indicative of the tolerance in most of the North and in the West. The South was slow to integrate. The all-white football team at Ole Miss, among many other institutionalized injustices, sparked race riots on campus as early as 1962. At Alabama, Bear Bryant allowed no African American players on his team until 1970. USC's prominence in that era was due, in part, to the recruiting of African American athletes in the South whom their own state universities wouldn't touch.

In the late sixties, groups such as the Black Panthers and the Student Nonviolent Coordinating Committee called for a revolution. Although their rhetoric was often idealistic, their actions were sometimes destructive. A 1969 "Free Huey Newton" rally at UCLA, organized by Black Panthers to protest the murder charges against Black Panther founder Huey Newton, resulted in horror. In a gun battle between rival factions of the Black Panthers' movement, two African Americans died.

In 1970, Black Panther leader Bobby Seale was tried in New Haven for the murder of a Panther believed to be a police informer. To prevent mayhem and ill will on campus, Yale University's president Kingman Brewster closed the university. Among the football players, the spirit of rebellion manifested itself in appearance. At Yale in 1970, Dick Jauron cultivated a mustache and shaggy locks. Before a vacation, Jauron's father, a former college football coach then living in Massachusetts, fetched his son and saw the transformation. He was silent for five blocks. Then he said, "There are leaders and there are followers. And let me tell you, I know a lot of followers with long hair."

When they arrived home, Jauron trimmed his hair and shaved his mustache.

At Michigan during that time, Bo Schembechler ordered his players to shave their mustaches. One African American player protested, saying that for him and for the other African American players, the mustache was a cultural necessity.

Schembechler swiftly amended his edict: all white players, he proclaimed, were to shave their mustaches, no buts about it. The African American athletes savored the small victory, but did not withdraw from the war. They couldn't. It raged all around them.

College students questioned everything, tested their teachers, met "because-I-said-so" pedantry with disgust. Football programs were often prototypes for this Socratic inversion. Players demanded that coaches justify all techniques, drills, policies, schedules, expectations, values, and choices regarding personnel. At times, they would not accept the explanations because they were too enraptured with the questioning.

In its 1969 fall football preview, *Sports Illustrated* listed John Pont's Indiana team as eleventh in the nation. Though they closed the 1968 season with an unremarkable 6–4 record, *Sports Illustrated* argued, many key games were near misses, Indiana falling 22–27 to Michigan and 35–38 to Purdue. Moreover, *Sports Illustrated* noted, nearly all the stars of the 1967 Rose Bowl team were entering their senior year, among them quarterback Harry Gonso, halfback John Isenbarger, and flanker Jade Butcher. The only Big Ten team ahead of Indiana in the 1969 rankings was the previous year's national champion, Ohio State, with eighteen of twenty-two returning starters.

In the opening game, Indiana easily wrested the Old Bourbon Barrel from Kentucky by a score of 58–30. Afterward, though, Pont's veterans faltered, falling 14–17 to California and 7–30 to Colorado. Response to those early defeats was a festering frustration. By the time Pont's team regained its footing, defeating Minnesota 17–7, Illinois 41–20, and Michigan State 16–0, morale had deflated. The spirit of the times offered a channel for the players' frustrations: ten African American athletes, citing discriminatory practices by the coaches, quit the team.

Gonso, Isenbarger, and Butcher were white.

Immediately after the shock caused by the accusations dissipated, Pont, in his most conciliatory fashion, extended an invitation for those ten athletes to return to their team.

As coach and players were reaching the climax of the tense, guarded, but reverberant negotiations, a separate crisis occurred. The Sigma Alpha Epsilon fraternity house, in which eleven Indiana football players resided, among them Harry Gonso, was destroyed by fire.

The ten African American athletes slapped away Pont's extended hand, rejecting the opportunity to return to the team.

If Pont had the power of Yale's president Kingman Brewster, perhaps he would have canceled the final games of the 1969 season in order first to inform the ten protesters that without them there could be no team, and second to force the Indiana community into reflection on racism. Pont had no such power, of course, just as he had no magic with which to show his disgruntled athletes that he did not think less of them for being black, just as they did not think less of him for being a "spik."

Indiana closed that 1969 season with three losses, falling 17–28 to Iowa, 27–30 to Northwestern, and 21–44 to Purdue, accumulating a 4–6 final record. Indiana, over the next three years, replicated exponentially those three dour games that drooped in the November 1969 chill. They staggered through three more losing seasons: 1–9 in 1970, 3–8 in 1971, 5–6 in 1972.

Though he was the first coach to guide Indiana to a bowl game, and the only one, still, to earn the right to play in the

Rose Bowl, Pont's success at Indiana had been infected by the turmoil of the times. Though he tried, he could not find a way to heal the program. So he chose to leave Bloomington to its basketball.

That, just then, the head coaching position at Northwestern opened was a boon to Pont and his family, who had become antsy in Bloomington. Because the Pont children knew their father was far better than circumstances allowed, they encouraged the move. Pont slid into his new job quite comfortably, especially after the powers that be assured him, in private, that he would soon acquire the plum of the athletic director's position.

The university provided the Ponts with a house near campus. Chicago provided them with a cosmopolitan setting. After Indiana, it seemed to be a dream come true.

But the dream was someone else's. Really, Pont was as out of his element at Northwestern as he had been when he first arrived at Yale. The experiences differed, though; while Yale welcomed him at once, Northwestern never did. Early on, university president Robert Strotz said he hoped Northwestern wouldn't get in the habit of going to the Rose Bowl because it might tarnish the university's academic image. Pont should have read that early warning sign: this couldn't be home.

Sandy Pont was expected to entertain Northwestern power brokers after the games. Once, on a Saturday when Pont's team squared off against his former employer, Indiana, the list of invitees doubled. Though the guests all showed up, the caterer did not. The Ponts called for Chinese takeout from the local restaurant.

It was a time of feast and famine. During a stint as coach of the country's college football all-stars in the East-West Shrine game in San Francisco, Pont took his family on a rare vacation, and they settled comfortably into the Fairmont Hotel. While her parents were out, Jennifer and another coach's daughter called room service and ordered lobster Newburg.

But back at Northwestern, the win column remained lean. After two 1–10 seasons, in 1976 and 1977, Pont called it quits as Northwestern's head coach, wishing to devote himself to victory, if not in football, then in other sports by devoting himself to the duties of athletic director.

The worst aspect of the decision must have been letting go of friends like Ernie Plank, who had been his assistant for years. Their kids had grown up with the Pont children, and with Pont's choice, the extended family was decimated. Pont's oldest son, John, told me that he was under the impression that at least one of the assistants was quite angry: he wanted to stick it out together at Northwestern no matter what.

When Northwestern let Pont go from his position as athletic director two years later, everyone must have realized that the situation at Northwestern allowed no one, no matter how committed, to stick it out and make it work.

While Pont clung to his job as athletic director, Nick Mourouzis, Pont's quarterback at Miami from 1956 to 1959, found life a little easier. He remained in his position as quarterback coach at Northwestern under Pont's successor, Rick Venturi. Just after Pont left Northwestern entirely, Mourouzis was offered an opportunity against which Pont's experience should have warned him: to be a head coach. But Mourouzis, during his twenty-three years as an assistant coach, a bulk of them as underling to Pont, had dreams. So he elected to be the boss: at DePauw University in Greencastle, Indiana. There, in twenty-one seasons, he has enjoyed a 121–74–4 record and a peaceful life in a town not unlike Oxford. It is a home.

Pont, though, was temporarily without one. Searching for new quarters, he first tried his hand at insurance; then at sales, peddling weight training equipment; then at the obligatory stint with television commentary. He remained restless. Pont still had the shirt on his back, but it wasn't a football jersey.

Pont must have thought that Mourouzis had the right idea. He heard about a job opening at a small college outside Cincinnati named Mount St. Joseph, a women's school turned coed, which planned to attract male candidates by starting a football program. When Pont applied, the president of the college, Francis Marie Thrailkill, must have felt God was playing on her team.

As soon as he was hired, Pont set to work. He sent out one thousand recruiting letters, designed and painted the school's first male locker room, and persuaded a local doctor to donate strength-training equipment. With his six part-time assistants, he worked out an athlete-friendly system of coaching. If a player knocked on the door of a staff meeting wanting to talk to Coach, that meeting quickly ended.

Pont's players won their season's opener 31–10 over Rose-Hulman. The following game, at home, was played on the field of a local high school; Mount St. Joseph's largest athletic field was ninety feet long.

The pressure-free environment of Mount St. Joseph was refreshing for Pont, reminding him of why he loved the game. In fact, he enjoyed building a program from scratch so much that he decided to take football on the road to a place it had never been before.

Since his days at Mount St. Joseph College, Pont has been in Tokyo, coaching for a semiprofessional team, the Gakusei Eigo Aei. Because their season spans only five games—taking on teams called Kajima Construction and Mitsubishi Bank—he is able to spend half the year in Japan and half in his home in Oxford, Ohio. He has assimilated Japanese culture well: his spoken Japanese is impeccable.

His players there refer to him as *Ojiisan,* grandfather, and to Sandy as *Obaasan,* grandmother. That, according to Pont's philosophy, is his measure of success as a coach, a much more important yardstick than his 85 percent winning record.

Sandy admitted to me that, after all these years, she still doesn't really know how to watch football. Because she is in Tokyo not to help her husband in his work as football missionary, but rather as a wife, I asked her how she got by; didn't she miss her grandchildren in the United States? But she takes cooking classes; she is *Obaasan* to an entire team of grown men. Japan has become another home.

On one trip back to the United States, Pont stayed long enough to have brain surgery. Then he returned to Japan to continue coaching.

John Pont's number 42 jersey was the first Miami ever retired. The shirt, though, is not the man. Even without that shirt on his back, I doubt John Pont could ever retire from football. That's the Ohio boy in him.

14

Character

When I told Esther Gillman that I was scheduled to interview Paul Dietzel, she acted as if I had just announced my impending marriage to Frankie Avalon. "Oh, Paul's *so* handsome," she proclaimed with that strange melding of objectivity and wistfulness women project when talking about an idol who's also a very real man.

Sources more detached than Esther have, almost without fail, commented on Dietzel's appearance. The opening sentence of a 1962 cover article in *Sports Illustrated* reads, "Paul Dietzel, young, tall, blond, lithe, and supercharged, leaped onto the stage of Thayer Hall at West Point...." Even a Baptist minister, writing in an essay celebrating Dietzel's commitment to Christ, can't resist remarking on his "boyish face." A fleet of different observers placed Dietzel's physical presence in the foreground of his coaching success. I wondered if the former caused the latter, both excited by and skeptical of the suggestion that such superficiality influenced the football world.

I couldn't wait to meet him.

Before traveling to Baton Rouge for that interview, I dredged up every picture of him I could find, especially those from his early years of coaching. In photos with other coaches, he stood at least half a head above those around him and was much less stout than all of them, not lean but stately. His hair was more brown than blond, except in direct sunlight, which blanched it to feathery whiteness. The omnipresent boyishness had an inviting charm. It was both happy and wise.

But it was overscrubbed. In one shot of him, flanked by a crew from Miami, among them Ara Parseghian and George Blackburn, Dietzel sported a Hawaiian shirt that made his stately presence a little corny. Yes, I decided, he was handsome, but not enough to deserve Esther Gillman's objective, wistful deification.

Dietzel, best I could guess, was a character. He's never done the expected thing: he went from Ohio to Louisiana, back north, back south. In the end, he retired to Beech Mountain, North Carolina, where he—of all things—paints watercolors. He teaches children to ski. He chose this hamlet because it is a place in Dixie blessed with an abundance of snow. Because his coaching career lugged him up and down so many times, he was able to reconcile the disparate qualities in this near balance of North and South.

Many forces played a role in molding his character. Bear Bryant in Kentucky, Sid Gillman in Ohio, and Red Blaik at West Point toughened and sharpened Dietzel's mind. On his own at LSU, though, his sharpness flashed, then dulled. In light of his 1958 success, the South couldn't help but spoil him and his teams. While his players grew apathetic to victory in the 1959 and the 1960 seasons—the 1959 team, most specifically, still containing the talent that earned Dietzel the national championship the year before, went 9–2—he reached beyond it. In this brief period of success and disillusionment emerged a new vision: a commitment to Christianity.

At first glance, football and Christianity might not seem analogous. But it was through LSU's chapter of the Fellowship of Christian Athletes that he was able to reconnect with his beliefs.

From among the many metaphors Jesus evokes for followers and interpreters, Dietzel chose to elevate the depiction of Christ as the quintessential worker. It was that aspect of Jesus's character that Dietzel consistently and most deliberately emulated. In all aspects of his life, he vowed never to give in to complacency.

"When you become a Christian," he said, "God sweeps your house clean, but webs and dirt will keep coming back.

I've found that I must constantly battle against temptation to keep myself under control."

While Dietzel was Colonel Blaik's assistant at Army, he established a method of recruiting suitable for the most monomaniacal of generals. For that reason, he was later wooed away from the south by West Point Superintendent General William C. Westmoreland. Though his success at LSU and his contacts supplied enough credentials for the Army position, Army's recent record under Dale Hall—particularly in regard to the three-year losing streak to Navy—demanded the hiring of an icon, not of national football, but of Army football. Though no nongraduate of West Point had become head coach since 1911, Dietzel had earned his football stripes there. Despite the brevity of his two stints at West Point, Dietzel was a rare star who shined with the pure light of Colonel Blaik's glory days. And unlike his West Point colleague Vince Lombardi, he had missed the horror of the 1951 cheating scandal, which drained ninety players from the program, among them Blaik's son Bob, a quarterback.

Above all, Dietzel, whose LSU teams never lost to their rival Tulane, was hired specifically to shut down Army's nemesis: Navy. In essence, he was called on to be Army's savior. He tried to be it through seemingly endless toil, putting in consistent sixteen-hour days.

But first, Dietzel had to break his contract with LSU. Politicos from Louisiana made a fuss in Washington over the loss of their coach, forgetting that they had bent some rules themselves to pull him away from his position as assistant to Colonel Blaik in 1955. Nevertheless, they incited Congress to put the heat on Westmoreland.

But their efforts to pressure Westmoreland and keep Dietzel proved unsuccessful, and in 1962 Dietzel returned to the site of his apprenticeship with Red Blaik, bringing with him the tricks of the trade he'd developed on his own. Though the gimmick might have seemed to some a little corny for West Point, Dietzel revived the Chinese Bandits. He arranged with John Martin, owner of the Bear Mountain Inn and a local fan of Army football, to secure 2,200 coolie hats in order to stage the comeback. The hats were placed in bags under the seats of the stadium; the band director learned the chant; when the Bandits hit the field, cadets and officers removed their uniform hats and became Dietzel's army.

But one can only work so hard, can only perfect a system so much. At some point, character has to come into play. No one can be entirely in control and objective when squaring off with the arch rival. Dietzel once said, "You can learn more character on the two-yard line than anywhere else in life." This lesson, it would seem, occurred for him during the 1963 Army-Navy game, Dietzel's second experience in that arena.

In his first, the year before, Army lost its contest to a Roger Staubach–led Navy 34–14. The following year, Dietzel invented a new system he called the Roger Staubach drill; instead of rushing Staubach, they held him in the pocket.

For most of that game, keeping Staubach in check was a strategy that worked. Deep into the game, Army and Navy were tied 7–7. Then Navy's running back Pat Donnelly scored two successive touchdowns to take his team up 21–7. But Army returned the favor. Army quarterback Rollie Stichweh put together a well-measured touchdown drive, also successfully executing a two-point conversion. The score was 21–15. With six minutes remaining in the game, Stichweh picked up the onside kick. With just over a minute and a half to play, Army still had the ball. The crowd was on their feet, generating a wall of noise. Stichweh completed a fourth-down pass to the Navy seven. With twenty seconds to play, they got the ball to the two-yard line. By then, the noise of the spectators had become unbearable. Stichweh requested that the ref quiet the crowd. For an instant, it worked. Then Army moved into formation and the roar resumed. Stopping the clock, the ref tried to reestablish quiet. He started the clock again. Once more, the noise resumed and Stichweh asked for the clock to be stopped.

By the time it was restarted—a third time—time had run out on the game and on Army.

A situation like that will challenge your character. It made Dietzel and his team stronger. They got their revenge the next season, defeating Navy 11–8.

After the following year's 7–7 tie with Navy, Dietzel began to feel the West Point administration was no longer as attentive to the needs of football as it had been during the Blaik years. So he followed up on an offer from South Carolina to be both coach and athletic director, taking on an entirely new kind of challenge.

The team was on probation; the football stadium was in complete disrepair; the athletic department had no money. As his first order of business, Dietzel took a behind-the-scenes approach to turning around the program: fund-raising. In short order, he secured the funds to construct one of the finest stadiums in the country.

Moreover, in 1969, he brought South Carolina the ACC championship and its first ever bowl bid. Unfortunately, the team lost that Peach Bowl game to West Virginia. That loss was characteristic. Between 1966 and 1974, Dietzel's team had only three winning seasons.

Soon, Dietzel felt that the university administration did not appreciate the Christian message implicit in many of his public addresses. When Dietzel stepped down from coaching in 1974, his athletic director position strangely vanished. Dietzel was allowed to stay on as a vice president, but the role didn't feel right, so he stepped down.

I cannot help but place coaches' records side by side for comparison. Dietzel and Parseghian, those sons of Gillman, offer a stunning contrast. Dietzel transformed LSU so early in his career and so emphatically, earning a national championship. Parseghian appeared to take longer, turning Northwestern around under the gaze of apathetic eyes. But then he did the same at universally scrutinized Notre Dame, successfully piloting the country's most visible program into the television era. Still peaking, still shrewd, charged, and intensely penetrating, he retired from the game. Now we remember Parseghian solely as a winner.

Dietzel, though, continued in football along a winding path. He became commissioner of Ohio Valley Conference athletics, athletic director at Indiana University, athletic director at LSU, and vice president at Samford University. At the outset of his career he jumped from position to position as assistant coach; his career ended with that same frenetic motion.

I wonder why Dietzel didn't follow his old teammate's lead in abandoning collegiate athletics sooner. I wonder why he meandered through old stomping grounds, playing roles that invited neither glory nor adrenaline rush, when he could have secured his deification if he had simply vanished from the football world.

But Parseghian scarcely chose to suspend his image at just the perfect moment, nor could Dietzel. It's not in his character. What some call work, for Dietzel, is an affirmation of his belief. If he ceases to move forward, he falters.

Even in 1996, he stood at a Fellowship of Christian Athletes conference alongside Bill Bradley to sing "Onward Christian Soldiers" and "Rise Up, O Men of God."

Years before, Bradley listened to a Fellowship of Christian Athletes album, on which Paul Dietzel's voice said, "We must be like the great athlete who just can't get enough coaching, who does everything possible to improve himself. That's the way we ought to play the game of life, under the Master Coach, Jesus Christ."

It's not corny when you believe in it.

I arrived early at the Coffee Call in Baton Rouge—the home of Dietzel's son Steve—where I was to meet Dietzel. Despite my study of photographs, in my heart of hearts I still anticipated a ringer for Burt Lancaster. So, when a tall, light-haired man with glasses and a quick chin weaved through the café, I hesitated. Though he matched a literal description of Dietzel, he wasn't the screen icon Esther Gillman's voice had compelled me to anticipate.

But he gazed on every patron in the place with a quivering smile as if in expectation of seeing, at long last, his oldest and dearest friend. His parted lips reined in a smile; his darting eyes brimmed with stories. In a corny pink jacket and cream-colored loafers, he was a southern Dick Van Dyke. I knew it was Dietzel, handsome because he was so giddily alive.

I addressed him. In a baritone sweetened by just a glaze of southern twang, he confirmed his identity. The accent suited him so well I couldn't help but wonder if he had been born in New Orleans or Natchez or Memphis, wrapped in swaddling clothes, placed in a reed basket, and magically guided up the Mississippi River, through its tributaries, to Mansfield, Ohio.

We nibbled beignets and sipped café au lait. He took me to his rented apartment where he acted out Billy Cannon catching a pass on the run and sang the Chinese Bandits chant. He and his lovely wife Anne treated me to a Cajun-style lunch.

There was no end to his excitement with everything he said and did. His energy was so high, I wondered why he finally left football. I can only guess that he found there was other work to be done.

15

Daughters

As my sisters and I grew up, we aspired merely to huddle under the beauty of Carm Cozza's daughters, Chris, Kathy, and Karen. On one rare occasion, my sister Mary succeeded. Mid-seventies, at a summer football camp on Cape Cod, low tide, Karen Cozza—svelte and raven haired—coaxed Mary to venture across the exposed sandbars as far as she could go. In shorts and Yale sweatshirt, her hair in a bun, Mary flung herself from sandy rise to sandy rise, digging her toes into the breath holes of burrowing shellfish. Quickly, Karen and Mary transformed into slim, dark silhouettes while the rest of the coaches' children watched in awe.

Finally, at the rumble of the incoming tide, they returned to us. Karen offered her slim hand, attentive to Mary's small-legged struggling, and Mary quivered in Pentecostal worship.

Safely back on the beach, though, Mary encountered a vaster image that suppressed all thought of Karen Cozza. Through the wall-length window of the dining hall, she saw the football players, hunched with exhaustion and pleasure over an early dinner. Some of them might have observed her and smiled, but it seemed to Mary that she watched them without reciprocity, as she should and always would. She couldn't believe how lucky she was.

Throughout the seventies, we all felt lucky. All the elegance and aplomb of Yale were wedded to victory. Between 1970 and 1979, Cozza's teams won or shared four Ivy League championships, and came in second place four times. There was only one losing season—1971—when Yale finished with a 4–5 record. But even that year, there was so much else to remember.

Mainly, there was Dick Jauron. Though the son of a former college coach known for his bluster, Jauron was a quiet, studious guy. Yet he rivaled Brian Dowling for cult-figure status. Coaches defended Jauron from tipsy fans who accosted him on the sidelines of games.

Cozza's players were groomed more for Wall Street than for professional football. Seeing Dick Jauron in his civilian clothes, one could easily imagine him a surgeon, which he had aspired to be before he was drafted by the Detroit Lions.

In 1972, his final season, his playing reached a storybook culmination in "The Game." Yale had not won in Cambridge in twelve years, and the 1972 matchup also began inauspiciously, with Yale trailing Harvard by 17–0 at halftime. In the third quarter, though, Dick Jauron scored two touchdowns— one on a seventy-four-yard run—launching a rally that resulted in a 28–17 Yale victory. After his 183-yard rushing day, Jauron finished that season with 1,055 rushing yards—a Yale record complemented by another he earned that day: twenty-eight career touchdowns.

Cozza soon found a replacement for Jauron who was as athletic and as dapper: Gary Fencik. That Fencik is now an investment banker is an Ivy League finish. Before getting there, though, Fencik took a detour through the Chicago Bears, for whom he was an all-pro defensive back, playing on their 1986 Super Bowl championship team. For Cozza, from 1973 to 1975, he was a stunning receiver.

At the 1975 Princeton game, Fencik took part in the longest pass play in Yale's football history. In the second quarter of the game, the score 0–0, Yale was scrambling on its own three-yard line. The quarterback, Stone Phillips, dropped back three yards into the end zone and pitched out to halfback Don Gesicki, who hit Fencik on the run. Ninety-seven yards later, Fencik put six points on the board.

He could catch anything. He set every possible Yale receiving record—most catches and most yards receiving in a game, season, career.

Then the Bears picked him up on waivers and turned him into a defensive end.

Two years later, John Spagnola stepped up to be Cozza's

star. He was a receiver to rival Gary Fencik, but that is not what impressed me most about him. Most fabulous was the depth of my sister's crush on him. She had scrapbooks filled with pictures and articles; she even had her picture taken with him. As far as any of the coaches' children were concerned, he was not just a football player: he was a teen idol.

Or as much of one as a Yale football player can be. The next year, when Spagnola was drafted by the Philadelphia Eagles, fellow player Rick Angelone went to his room to congratulate him. He found Spagnola fast asleep, exhausted from pulling an all-nighter to study for a political science exam.

Spagnola's move to the Eagles did not signal an end to Cozza's success. The 1970s decade of dreams spilled over into the next. In 1980, Yale upset Air Force 17–16 for Cozza's one hundredth win. Captain John Nitti reported that, in the locker room at halftime, trailing Air Force, they collectively vowed to win that game for their coach.

The following year, energized by running back Rich Diana, Yale scored another upset, this time over Navy, 23–19. Cozza won that game for himself, he stated after the game, to impress former coach Ara Parseghian, who was in the press box reporting for ABC.

But at the close of the 1981 season, in which Yale secured its third straight Ivy League title, a curtain fell.

To those of us who, throughout the seventies, pulsed in the heart of sold-out Yale Bowl crowds, the lean eighties and nineties often felt like nuclear winter. The encroaching frost transformed fans' attitude from smug to belligerent. When Yale was winning, they took credit; when Yale was losing, they blamed Cozza, the rest of the staff, the players.

Perhaps the media was responsible for the struggles of the eighties and early nineties. The division between I-A and I-AA schools offered them an unquestionable means to differentiate between marketable and unmarketable games. Even the historic matchup of Yale and Harvard, regardless of sometimes great records and always deep emotions, could never preempt parallel contests between Michigan and Ohio State, Florida and Florida State, Mississippi and Mississippi State, even Indiana and Purdue, that all fall, every year, on the same Saturday in late November. So why would any athlete, no matter how intelligent, choose to play football, pay tuition, and accept anonymity at Yale rather than accepting a full scholarship to light up a nation of TV screens in a Michigan uniform?

Cozza, though, points to the academic index as the culprit. The AI, as it is sometimes called, established in 1981, defined base-level academic standards that high school athletes must meet to be considered for acceptance to Ivy League schools. At all eight universities, those standards are lower than those applied to the general pool of applicants. However, from university to university, there is tremendous disparity among those standards.

It's easy to tinker with the AI. It is a numerical average of class rank, GPA, and standardized test scores. A perfect score in each area is 80. To qualify for consideration at any Ivy League school, a candidate must reach 161 on the AI. Each school differs, though, on how many athletes will be accepted whose AI ranking hovers around that 161 cutoff. Penn and Cornell take the most, while Harvard, Yale, and Princeton accept the least.

Yale's president Bart Giamatti anticipated the establishment of the AI with a foreboding message he delivered to a group of alumni in the spring of 1981, which has since been labeled the "deemphasis" speech.

Cozza, at first, read that speech as a statement of purpose to lessen the visibility and therefore the success of the athletic programs.

Later he decided that he—and the rest of the world—misunderstood Giamatti's intent. Really, he was restating, in general, Yale's position on athletics, and affirming his commitment to live by those expectations. Moreover, it was a challenge to other Ivy League presidents to rein in athletic programs that were moving toward professionalism.

Though some credit Giamatti's speech for inspiring the AI, Cozza dismisses that notion, citing, rather, a notable lowering of academic standards in Princeton's and Penn's basketball programs.

Those athletic programs were intensely plugged into a changing world. They knew what buttered their bread. Penn basketball coach Steve Bilsky learned from the admissions office that a prospective student from Nebraska had not heard of Penn until he saw Penn play Nebraska in the NCAA tournament. Bilsky articulated an unfortunate truth: "Television... you can't overstate its importance."

This mercenary point of view created the AI imbalance in the Ivy League. For several years in the early nineties, this discrepancy was perfectly mirrored in won-loss records.

In short, Penn dominated football in the Ivy League.

"Everybody thinks we're breaking some rules," said former Penn quarterback Mark DeRosa. "I'm sure we're bending some rules, but everybody else better start bending some, too."

Cozza, though, was an honest guy. Playing by Cozza's rules, my father recruited players largely from Ohio and its surrounding states. He kept a Rolodex with a card for each recruit, containing name, height, weight, class rank, GPA, SAT and/or ACT scores. Sometimes, I would thumb through the data, trying to divine the next Dick Jauron. I often found, to my dismay, that there was an inverse relationship between size and academic prowess. I worried for my father.

I worried for other reasons, too. Each year, my father vanished on the first day of hunting season—also the day the NCAA determined to be the opening of college football recruiting season. At suppertime every night in December, he called from towns of which I had never heard. I wondered how he could have possibly found football players in those towns, let alone found the towns themselves.

But I never fully appreciated the difficulty of this endeavor until I was in graduate school at Penn State. On his way to Ohio, my father stopped in State College to see me. Early in the morning on that first day of hunting season, I met him at the Nittany Lion Inn for breakfast. While walking through the lobby, we peeked into a reception room that was full of boys, some seated, some standing, all tall and muscular. We read the sign outside the door: PENN STATE RECRUITING BREAKFAST.

My father looked back at that herd of boys, then at me. At that moment, Joe Paterno had as many sons as he wanted, but my father had just one daughter.

Over time, there developed an unavoidable tension between daughters and football. Far beyond the schoolgirl crush my sister felt for John Spagnola, there came the grimmer reality of romance. Once, when Karen Cozza crashed a Yale mixer, quarterback Bob Rizzo asked her to dance. For a while, they had a fine time, till one of Rizzo's friends tipped him off as to the identity of his dancing partner. "Pretend this never happened," said Rizzo. But Karen didn't; she let her father know that she was a little upset that football had gotten in the way of her social life.

I know how Cozza loved his daughters. But the older and more Sophia Loren–like they became, the more Cozza's life with football suffered. No amount of beauty can assuage losing. During games in the eighties and early nineties, the Cozza daughters sat face-forward in the nearly empty stands, watching the game, but conscious that things had changed.

In hindsight, Cozza wishes he'd retired in 1994, a year in which Yale defeated both the University of Connecticut and Harvard. Then, he could have made his announcement, his daughters standing beside him in one last glow of victory.

But Cozza elected to step down for good at the close of his

thirty-second season, in 1996. The 30–0 victory over Brown in the opening game of that season suggested his team would give him a much-deserved send-off. Then injuries scourged the team, causing six straight losses and an average of eighty-five rushing yards per game.

His only crime as a coach was that his team had done too well for just long enough to spoil its fans. Loss, even when imposed by circumstances beyond control, was unacceptable, fueling nearly a decade of defensiveness.

Cozza, by that point, appeared isolated from his former Miami cronies. Though Bill Mallory had served on his coaching staff in 1965, he retreated to Ohio. Of three other Miami graduates who acted as Cozza's assistants in the early part of his Yale career—Jim Root, Bill Narduzzi, and Seb LaSpina—only LaSpina remained through the bluer years. And there to give Cozza comfort, too, was his old roommate John Pont's little brother, Rich.

Strange how rapidly Cozza's replacement, Jack Siedlecki, changed Yale football's blue mood. He turned Yale's program around in three years, leading them to an Ivy League championship in 1999. Or perhaps not so strange. During the 1999 game against Dartmouth, in front of a homecoming crowd, a Yale player, early in the game, came off the field after a botched series of downs. He took off his helmet and shouted, "What the fuck are we doing out there!" He was loud enough for everyone in the Yale stands to hear.

The image of that player was as different from that of

Cozza's three daughters as it could possibly be. You would never hear foul language on the field when Cozza coached. I guess that was the problem. For a decade, Yale lived a dreamy ideal where athletes pulled all-nighters to study, and the daughters of coaches were too precious to dance with. Now, I suppose, Yale is getting real.

16

Heart

Woody Hayes's joys and troubles flowed in his diabetic blood while Bo Schembechler's churned in his heart.

While Schembechler was recovering from his first heart attack in 1969 in California, just before the Rose Bowl, Millie and Bo's infant son Shemy joined him there. Back in Ann Arbor, assistant coach Larry Smith and his wife Cheryl took care of the three older boys. Nine months later, Cheryl gave birth to a son, Toby, who had been conceived in the Schembechlers' bed.

Who can't connect the heart with love?

So great was his love for football that the heart attack preceding Schembechler's first Rose Bowl visit did not inspire him to change his work habits, nor did the queasiness he felt six years later after playing a brisk game of racquetball, but the excruciating pain he experienced during the Minnesota game in November of 1987 and the open-heart surgery that followed made him wake up.

In December, he announced his retirement.

But, because of some weakness of the heart, it took him another two seasons to follow through on it.

What was Bo Schembechler without his football? What was his family without their father and football?

Bo loved Millie and her children from a previous marriage. He adopted her three sons, Chip, Geoff, and Matt, and the only son they conceived together, Shemy, grew up regarding the three as his brothers. Millie loved Bo. But she didn't need him; she could give him up to football. That, I think, is what Bo loved best about her.

Looking back, Shemy Schembechler still can't figure out why he stopped playing football. I know why. It's more interesting to watch.

Moreover, Shemy, like the rest of his family, was really so close to his father's game that I suspect he sometimes felt he was playing. When he was a student at Miami, his father's alma mater, he took a public speaking class. For one assignment, he recited a song penned by a sports announcer known in and around Ann Arbor as "The Voice of Michigan Football." To this day, Shemy has perfect recall of the piece; he did an impromptu performance for me over dinner in Chicago.

> Ohio came to bury Michigan
> all wrapped in maize and blue.
> The words were said,

the prayers were read,

and everybody cried.

But when they closed the coffin,

there was someone else inside.

Ohio came to bury Michigan,

but Michigan wasn't dead,

and when that day was over

it was someone else instead.

Twenty-two Michigan wolverines

took on the hoards of gray,

and, as Cavender played "The Victors,"

they laid Woody Hayes away.

That Shemy could recite that song illustrated for me not only his love for his father and for football, but also his sense that his father's greatness was contingent on his connection to Woody Hayes.

Schembechler emerged from the Ten-Year War the slim victor over Hayes, with a 5–4–1 record. After his mentor left the game, Schembechler drove his team through another decade of winning season after winning season. He produced his portion of professional players as well as a handful of coaches. He's not so sure that the coaching legacy of which he is a part still continues.

Though Schembechler coached ten more years after Hayes's retirement, continuing to produce much the same results, the story line seemed to end; much of the magic was gone. Michigan's powers of winning fizzled before its postseason game, without the excuse that they expended all their energy on their final Ohio State game. For the decade of the eighties, Schembechler was haunted by the specter of his friend, but it was a ghost only he could see.

For a decade, the Ohio State game had been Michigan's most important. Against that contest, the importance of postseason games paled. But even with the departure of Hayes, Schembechler's bowl game record continued to sag. After a 23–6 victory over Washington in the 1981 Rose Bowl, he fell into his characteristic slump.

Then, after his heart attack during the 1987 Minnesota game, his team owed him something. After all, they had put him through a great deal of physical turmoil. But because Schembechler's surgery took him away from the team's Hall of Fame Bowl preparations, the site of justice and reparations had to wait until the following year in the most perfect of settings: the 1989 Rose Bowl on January 1.

Michigan's team went to that game as 1988 Big Ten champions, with an outside chance at a national championship if Michigan took down USC and several upsets and/or ties concluded other January 1 bowl games. But USC's offensive attack was led by Heisman runner-up Rodney Peete, which did not bode well for Schembechler's team.

Quarterback Demetrius Brown, particularly, might have felt a bit of guilt over Schembechler's most recent attack; during that Minnesota game, he dislocated his thumb. He started the Rose Bowl game strong; on the fourth play of Michigan's first possession, Brown completed a twenty-one-yard pass to John Kolesar. Though USC's defense stopped them shy of a touchdown, Mike Gillette launched a forty-nine-yard field goal to give Michigan the early lead with 4:07 remaining in the quarter.

However, the auspicious start for Michigan was short-lived. Throughout the remainder of the first half, the teams struggled for domination, each turning the ball over once. Finally, USC's Peete capped off the first half with first a one-yard run for the game's initial touchdown, followed by a four-yard run to give USC a substantial 14–3 advantage.

The second half opened with mixed results for Michigan, with Brown completing a six-yard pass to Chris Calloway for a touchdown but failing to execute a two-point conversion. Then, at the close of the third quarter, Michigan drove ninety-two yards for its second touchdown of the game, scoring on a Brown pass, but again missing the two-point conversion. Michigan entered the fourth quarter with a precarious 15–14 edge.

But with less than six minutes remaining in the game, Michigan acquired a demeanor unusual in their Rose Bowl appearances. They drove for seven more points, then handily stopped USC as linebacker John Milligan picked off a Peete pass. In sealing the win, the players had done their part in paying back their coach.

Unfortunately, the other top-ranked teams were not as co-operative, so that Rose Bowl left Schembechler's team only fourth in the final national polls. Time was running out on the coach's quest for the elusive national championship. The press enjoyed some jokes at his expense, suggesting that Schembechler, as athletic director, should take credit for Steve Fisher's basketball championship, as Schembechler had been responsible for hiring Fisher. *Sports Illustrated* reported that Schembechler, after the NCAA basketball tournament finals, said dreamily, "Maybe, just maybe, we can carry it over into the fall."

But Schembechler's second-ranked team early in the season faced the Notre Dame team that stymied Nehlen's West Virginia squad in the Fiesta Bowl and took home the national championship.

Michigan had resumed its rivalry with Notre Dame under Schembechler's tenure, in 1978. From Schembechler's point of view, the renewal was auspicious: they beat Notre Dame 28–14 despite the fact that their quarterback Rick Leach had a bad ankle, and Notre Dame was led by Joe Montana. But the eighties' sun did not continue to shine like maize on Ann Arbor, and by the fall of 1989, the two teams' record against each other was 4–5 in Notre Dame's favor.

To make matters worse, on the field that September in 1989, Michigan faced a Notre Dame squad that numbered among its ranks Raghib "Rocket" Ismail. That Ismail scored on two kickoff returns facilitated a Notre Dame victory of 24–19. It was Michigan's only loss that season, except for the Rose Bowl game, in which they fell to USC 17–10. After that, Schembechler retired.

So the eighties was a decade of greatness ever so subtly undermined. Perhaps because of the absence of Hayes, Schembechler's continued contribution to the sport, during that time, was best viewed off the field.

Schembechler fought to keep his athletes in school, attending classes, getting the grades to succeed anywhere in life. He kept his recruiting clean. A proponent of Proposition 48, which set minimum standards for the academic admission of athletes, Schembechler nevertheless took risks on some kids who he believed could make it, then made sure they did.

Running back Gil Chapman, whose test scores were lower than Prop 48 specifications, made it through Michigan and afterward received his MBA from Rutgers. Defensive back Mike Harden was not accepted initially, but Schembechler persuaded the university to take a chance. Harden earned his degree in political science before joining the Denver Broncos.

But Schembechler's greatest football legacy might very well be Shemy. He looks almost too much like his father. Though he did not play football while at Miami, he is now as involved in the game as his father ever was: as a scout for the Chicago Bears. What he loves most about his job is the history of the Bears, as rich as any in football. When I visited him in the Bears offices, he pointed to a statue of former coach George Halas with such pride he might as well have been pointing to a statue of his own father.

Underneath all great loves, a sadness simmers. At some point, in a moment of strange quiet, it boils up and ruptures the paved surface of love's terrain. In football, there's always a way to solve a problem. In love there are fewer options.

Especially when you love in the public eye.

Schembechler's relationship with football didn't sit as well with son Matt as it did with the rest of the family. An article in the September 1999 issue of *Gentlemen's Quarterly* entitled "Bully Bo," written by Elwood Reid, spewed Matt's vitriol toward his father.

Really, though, the article seems to be about Reid's writer's block: he can't get past the material that he used for his first book, a novel in which he thinly veils his two-year experience as a Michigan player. Reid reported, "I figured [Matt Schembechler] has an ax to grind. And maybe I do too, because the truth is that Bo never left me. Even now I can hear his voice, feel the snap of his gaze as I stand in judgment before him." But Reid went too far in the article's supposedly nonfiction analysis, playing psychiatrist, suggesting Matt's suicidal tendencies were the direct result of his father.

Sure, Schembechler had a temper. In 1973, after Michigan and Ohio State tied each other 10–10—tying their conference records—and Big Ten athletic directors chose to send Ohio State to the Rose Bowl despite their appearance in Pasadena the previous year, Schembechler made a horrible stink. He was hard on the press, demanding of his athletes. But he was never underhanded, and he was always up front about who he was. He observed about himself: "They'll say he was an old, hard-nosed bastard, but that he was honest."

So Reid's work of fiction seems more true than the *Gentlemen's Quarterly* exposé that portrays Schembechler as a man without love for his sons.

Raising a son is no easy thing. When Shemy was four years old, he and his father had a telling exchange. Father asked son a question, but received no response. When Schembechler repeated himself, he again received no response. After the fourth address, in which he asked Shemy why he wouldn't respond, Shemy said, "Because you don't answer me when I talk to you."

That exchange must have changed Schembechler, because from then on wherever he went, Shemy went; he tucked Shemy deep inside his life.

I swear, Schembechler loved football, but he cared, above all, about his sons. I suspect that *GQ* article could have broken his heart.

But it didn't. After Millie died of adrenal cancer in 1992, those around Schembechler were unsure his heart would ever recover. Four years later, though, he remarried—a woman named Cathy Aikens, who makes sure her husband takes care of his health. When I first met him and he offered me cookies, I felt just from his presence the strength of his heart.

A few months later, my father and I attended the 2000 Walter Camp Awards dinner in order to watch Schembechler receive a lifetime achievement award. Schembechler and my father chatted about high school games they'd seen each other play, offering details so glibly it seemed that those games had just been played moments before; it seemed that they were two kids who just couldn't get enough of the game of football, their joy was that profound and complete.

When my father and I walked away from the conversation, he shook his head, marveling. He said, "I can't believe Bo. He hasn't aged a bit."

I guess it's that heart.

17

One Scrappy Kid

Bill Mallory keeps horses, always has, wherever he's lived. He hitches them up to carts, buggies, and sleighs. When I first met him, he was riding a tractor mower with a snow-plow attachment while two dogs loped behind. Though it was a brisk, snow-spackled day in Bloomington, Indiana, he was coatless. In his plaid shirt, vest, and corduroy trousers, he seemed perfectly content.

At first glance, he seemed to possess the unquestionable toughness of John Wayne. He spoke to me, though, with the gentlest affection. He expressed his respect for my uncle John Pont, but was uncertain as to whether he had met my father.

"Yes," I informed him. "After Bill Narduzzi's funeral, you and my Dad had a beer."

Mallory's face darkened as he remembered Narduzzi, who graduated from Miami two years after he had, and who was named NCAA Division II Coach of the Year in 1979, when his Youngstown State team lost to Delaware in the national finals. In the early seventies, when Narduzzi was, briefly, my father's colleague on the Yale staff, I played in his backyard.

When Mallory looked at me again, his face brightened. He seemed aware, as I was, of all the football between us. He led me into his home.

The house, with its exposed wooden beams, was just like him. He seems to be a man strong enough to hoist, Atlas-like, almost any football program on his shoulders and keep it there for eternity. But football is not as stable an entity as the world.

Colorado, first off, was too heavy.

The philosophy at the University of Colorado, Bill Mallory learned, was "win at any cost," turning a blind eye to illegal recruiting and grade massaging. This was the antithesis of the ideals Hayes and his other mentors had instilled in him. A rift between the athletic administrators and Mallory spread until, in a move characteristic of the Colorado athletic department, they fired Mallory to make way for New England Patriots coach Chuck Fairbanks, whom they not-so-surreptitiously wooed to Boulder. The university was ordered to pay $300,000 in damages to the Patriots for encouraging Fairbanks to break his contract.

Though Mallory steered his career away from systems like that at Colorado, he couldn't get away from the protean nature of football programs. After a few years at Indiana he discovered that it was, strangely, too light to hold up. Expectations were so low that he was named Big Ten Coach of the Year in 1986 for guiding Indiana to a 6–6 season.

Nineteen eighty-seven, Mallory's defining season at Indiana, in which he did what no one in his position had been able to do for thirty-five years—defeat Ohio State in Columbus—offered an omen. It came in the form of Earle Bruce, Ohio State's head coach since 1979, who had been Mallory's fellow assistant under Woody Hayes from 1966 to 1968. In 1987, Bruce's record since replacing Hayes was 81–26–1, better than any other active Big Ten coach at that time; he was undefeated in his first season, before taking his team to the Rose Bowl. In the world of high-power football programs, though, amnesia erases loyalty. Because his 1987 record of 6–4–1 didn't measure up, he was fired.

In 1988, Mallory was far from that fate. For the first time since 1904, Indiana defeated Ohio State in Bloomington. Then on December 28, 1988, in the Liberty Bowl they dominated South Carolina 34–10. Indiana finished the season 8–3–1; they were ranked twentieth in the nation.

The bright light of the 1989 season was Anthony Thompson, an earnest kid from Terre Haute, Indiana. He was third in the NCAA record books with 65 career touchdowns and 394 career points. His talent eclipsed the team's bad luck: two close losses, 14–17 against Kentucky and 31–35 against Ohio State. Nevertheless, as they went into their final game against Purdue with a 5–5 record, they were being considered for an invitation to the Freedom Bowl. Because Purdue's record at that time was 2–8, Mallory looked to close Indiana's fourth straight season with a bowl game.

Thompson appeared to be the man to lead the way. Near the end of the game, with Indiana behind 15–14, a Purdue kickoff landed in Thompson's arms at the Indiana twenty-one-yard line. He evaded one defender, then sped down the sidelines. He seemed destined for the goal. Then, at the Purdue fifteen-yard line, a safety cut at just the right angle to shove Thompson out of bounds.

His luck ended. Thompson ran the ball three more times, for a loss of one yard. Freshman Scott Bonnell attempted the field goal, but it was wide left. The clock ran out on Indiana's bowl bid.

One man, it seemed, couldn't always carry a team.

On December 2, during the Indiana-Kentucky basketball game in the Hoosier Dome, the announcement that Thompson finished second in the Heisman voting behind Houston's Andre Ware aroused a cacophony of booing. Indiana was beginning to feel like the Rodney Dangerfield of the football world. Thompson's only regret was that he couldn't give the Heisman Trophy to his mother.

Mallory, though, could not fail to celebrate this man. He retired Thompson's number—32—at the end-of-the-year banquet. Of all Indiana athletes, he was, at that time, the only one to receive that honor.

In 1991, Mallory had another man, Vaughn Dunbar. With

Dunbar's consistent rushing, Indiana reclaimed its stature, somewhat. Defeating Kentucky, Purdue, and Michigan State earned Indiana the coveted symbols of three long-standing rivalries: the Old Bourbon Barrel, the Old Oaken Bucket, and the Old Brass Spittoon. Michigan State was so dismissive of Indiana that they did not bring the Old Brass Spittoon to Bloomington, where they were defeated. Mallory claimed he would send an assistant coach up to get it if it wasn't shipped.

It was shipped... to the University of Iowa.

Mallory received another slap in the face. Big Ten commissioners suspended Mallory for one game because he criticized officials in a press conference after his 24–16 loss to Michigan. Two weeks later, Mallory traveled with his players to Madison for their matchup against Wisconsin, but departed two hours before the game for the journey home. Without their coach, Indiana won 28–20.

At the end of the season, Indiana's solid 6–4–1 season earned them a berth in the Copper Bowl in which Indiana defeated Baylor 24–0.

In 1993, receiver Thomas Lewis carried the team to an 8–3 regular season record and a trip to the Independence Bowl, where they met Virginia Tech. Although Lewis caught six passes for 177 yards and two touchdowns, his team gave up two touchdowns with thirty-five seconds left in the game. They lost 45–20.

That one man defined his team was something Mallory could not have wanted or promoted. He openly professed that he despised an "I" attitude, favoring effort over reputation. He gave scholarships to any walk-on that earned his keep. He was both tough and gentle with everyone.

But the fact remains that he was achieving his sporadic years of success by the scrappiness, luck, and oddball personalities of his players. With those types of athletes, Mallory, without undermining his feelings about equality on a team, worked magic.

No one epitomized that type more than Alex Smith.

Smith was a down-home kid who might have baffled a coach other than Mallory. His aspiration was to buy the Indiana county in which he lived and make the entirety a haven for hunters. Mallory, rider of horses, could meet Smith on his level.

In the first game of his freshman year, 1994, against Cincinnati, Smith rushed for 152 yards on twenty-three carries to seal a 28–3 victory. In the final game of the season, he broke the Big Ten freshman record with a total of 245 yards rushing in a 33–29 win over Purdue, supplying Mallory the tie for the lead in all-time Indiana coaching victories and giving Indiana a 7–4 record. After the season ended, Smith was named UPI freshman of the year. He seemed like the one man who could do it all for four years.

But during preseason practices in 1995, Smith pulled a hamstring, causing him to miss the opening game against Western Michigan. In the fourth game of the season, against Northwestern, when a defender tackled him, his shoulder pads slid upward, leaving his chest and back vulnerable. He broke three ribs. His luck, it seemed, had run out.

Smith missed three more games and wore cumbersome padding when he returned. Indiana closed the season 2–9, losing to every Big Ten team they met.

The Big Ten losing streak, lasting fourteen games, continued into 1996.

On October 31, after the thirteenth, a 48–26 loss to Penn State, athletic director Clarence Doninger called a press conference to announce that Bill Mallory was fired, but would coach the final three games of the season.

Shocked, Mallory strained to hold back the tears. At times during his tenure, he struggled, but he also had successes that, in number, surpassed any previous Indiana coach. But even the Indiana administration had little respect for all Mallory had done, treating him as if he were just one man in a whole world of men: insignificant, expendable.

His players didn't see him that way. They saw him as I did: an icon of strength, a well of caring. The announcement broke their hearts. "I hate to see him go," said Adewale Ogunleye. "I'm sorry it has to come down to winning and losing. I love him."

I attended the Indiana–Penn State game that sealed Mallory's fate. Though I earned my graduate degree from Penn State, I sat on the Indiana side of the stadium with my husband, sister, and brother-in-law because my father had acquired tickets through Indiana contacts. My brother-in-law was gleeful at Penn State's decimation of Indiana, loudly cheering while the Indiana fans around us fell into stony silence. During that game, though, I became an Indiana fan, empathic with the pain of losing. Though, at that time, I knew little about Mallory, I sensed the loss was ominous.

Two weeks after the Penn State debacle, a brokenhearted Indiana team fell to Ohio State 27–17.

But for the following week's game against Purdue, the last of Mallory's career, his players mended their hearts. With 5:11 left in the first half, Indiana defensive back Kywin Supernaw intercepted a pass deep in Purdue territory, then carried it for a touchdown, tying the score 10–10. Though Purdue moved ahead 16–10 by halftime, for the final two quarters, Indiana's defense held them scoreless. In their zeal, the defense forced four more turnovers, a blocked kick that led to a touchdown and three more pass interceptions. The defense accumulated a total of sixteen points, two earned by a safety in which three Indiana men sacked the Purdue quarterback in the end zone. When the clock ran out on a 33–16 Indiana victory, Mallory's team hoisted him on their shoulders and carried him off the field as if he were light as air.

Indiana's football team has failed to have a winning season since.

Mallory's wife Ellie had prepared herself for a day like October 31, 1996. In fact, she had built a fortress. In 1988, she was chatting over doughnuts with the wives of coaches from Baylor, LSU, Brigham Young, and the University of Washington at the national convention of the American Football

Coaches Association. They shared stories about the tumult of
the wife of a football coach. The topics were common: absent
husbands, hostile fans, the tedium of moving, the omnipresent fear that losing will ruin their lives.

Ellie had been uprooted from seven different homes; she
once chewed out a spectator for bad-mouthing Bo Schembechler; she felt deeply the long absences of her husband.
One December in Columbus, when her husband had em-
barked on the long journey of recruiting for Ohio State, she
was nursing three children through a bad case of the chicken
pox and couldn't do the Christmas shopping.

That conversation over coffee evolved into the founding of
the American Football Coaches Wives Association, a support
group for women whose husbands lead a life comparable to a
ticking bomb.

In *When Pride Still Mattered,* David Maraniss's biography
of Vince Lombardi, Maraniss depicts the legendary coach's
relationship with his wife Marie as sad at best. That he was
obsessed with and she was disinterested in football made
their relationship so strained that she drank heavily, became
depressed, and ignored her children, while her husband as-
cended to the heights of a football Olympus. They shared
little except their last name.

Marie Lombardi was not typical of coaches' wives. Others,
like Esther Gillman, who began dating Sid when she was in
high school and has been married to him for more than sixty
years, thrived on the frenetic, stimulating lifestyle football
created. Esther, Ellie Mallory, and their compatriots were

deeply committed to their husbands, their husbands' teams, individual players, the universities for which their husbands worked. It was that intensity of involvement that made football so stressful.

So Ellie, an elected officer in the safe haven of the American Football Coaches Wives Association, was well buttressed when Doninger dropped the ax on her husband. And despite the fact that her husband has been out of football for several years, she is just now considering retirement from that organization.

At Mallory's retirement dinner, his team presented him with the mower he was riding when I first saw him. They wanted to give him a horse, but that gift would have been much more pricy, and he had, after all, been fired.

That money dictates a bulk of the action in the world of football is a concept that Mallory could never shoulder, not because it is too heavy or too ephemeral, but because he can't see it. He sees only people.

One rock star lives in Indiana: John Mellencamp. He lives, not in a pink house, but in a mansion a ways down the road from the Mallorys in Bloomington. In 1996, Indiana University dedicated the Mellencamp Pavillion, which was built with money he donated to the football program for an indoor practice facility.

That advancement was a symbol that the era of Mallory had ended. A coach like Mallory would, in a heartbeat, trade all the modern innovations in the world for just one more scrappy kid.

18

The Press

In 1999, while West Virginia succumbed to Navy 31–28, a single-engine plane buzzed over the stadium. Trailing behind it was a banner that read: DON NEHLEN MUST GO.

On his birthday, Merry Ann Nehlen baked her husband a cake, which she decorated with an edible version of that plane, complete with banner.

They couldn't give credence to such criticism or, as Nehlen put it, "I'd go wacko." To close off the criticism entirely, particularly in a fragile circumstance like Nehlen had at West Virginia, required an opaque faith that acted as offensive line against the press of the press.

West Virginia is a cheap and easy target. While in Penn State's graduate school, I learned to regard Morgantown, West Virginia, as a suburb of Pittsburgh. Both a map and a stray West Virginia football roster, with many a Pennsylvania hometown listed beside the players' names, supported this belief. Moreover, to get to Morgantown, I needed to fly to Pittsburgh.

When I started driving south, though, the landscape changed. The hills rose like bread, their tops windburned and bare. The valleys cradled mist and purple shadows. The few houses that I saw were huddled against the hillsides. The road, even when ascending, felt like it was descending.

Morgantown is Brigadoon, removed in space and time from Pennsylvania and every place beyond.

If Don Nehlen is responsible for maintaining the purity of his town, his university, and his program, he would never say so. He is far too interested in praising his football brethren from Ohio.

He is very angry about the way Indiana treated Bill Mallory.

The sons of Doyt Perry, Woody Hayes, and Sid Gillman have some power to make each other's lives easier. After all, when Nehlen lost his position as head coach at Bowling Green, Bo Schembechler hired him as a Michigan assistant. Above all there is empathy. When I asked Bo Schembechler what he thought "greatness" in a coach meant, he responded that it meant grappling with a difficult situation. Certainly, the persistence of Mallory at Indiana and Nehlen at West Virginia qualified them for greatness. But even if they accepted Schembechler's definition, the frustration did not go away, and no one, not even Schembechler or every coach together, could make it do so.

I asked Nehlen if he was considering retirement. His clipped response of "No" sounded like a statement prepared to stymie journalists trying to dig up dirt.

I was hurt. I felt I deserved more.

Any coach is kin to my father; any coach from Ohio is his brother. With Don Nehlen—from Canton, from Bowling Green—I expected to see my father sitting in his chair.

Nehlen has more hair, a little more height, paler skin and eyes, but otherwise his presence is that of my father. He sits very still. He holds up pinkie, index, and middle finger to illustrate the count of three. He reports the positive and the negative with equal emotion—a poker face—a face of idealism or of cynicism... I wasn't sure.

His gambling career at West Virginia continued longer than any preceding coach, even Bobby Bowden, who led the team from 1970 to 1975. The peculiarity of the setting never allowed him to establish a real dynasty in which success built upon itself. Rather, he continued to play a penny-ante game in which he hoped for a decent deal.

In 1988, he got a hand as good as that which he held with Jeff Hostetler. His hole card was Major Harris, a Pittsburgh native who somehow slipped through the fingers of Pitt coach Foge Fazio and found himself in a place as unlike his neighborhood in Pittsburgh as it could possibly be. Though the Hill District was a den of crime and temptation, Harris never took a puff from a cigarette nor a sip of hard alcohol. He sampled beer, but decided he didn't like it.

Really, he seemed well suited for West Virginia, that Nehlen-maintained Brigadoon. Luck guided him as it had all of Nehlen's career.

Take, as an example, a particular play against the giant from the north, Penn State. On first and ten from the Penn State twenty-six, with no score in the first quarter, Harris found himself in a broken play. The rest of the West Virginia offense went left; Harris went right, where only he and five Penn State defenders remained. Harris cut back hard, evading the rush, and waltzed across the goal line, setting the tone for an unbelievable 51–30 upset.

As the special team rushed onto the field, Harris returned to the sideline and confessed to Nehlen, "My fault, coach."

Nehlen informed Harris that he could live with it.

That naïveté conjured a dream of a national championship for West Virginia. Then the dream approached a reality. Unbeaten West Virginia, ranked third in the country, was set to face Lou Holtz's also unbeaten, top-ranked Notre Dame squad in the Fiesta Bowl. Each team hoped to emerge national champion.

But this was a dream from which West Virginia eventually woke. The reality that prodded Nehlen's team from its dream manifested itself in the form of Holtz, then strangely transformed into themselves.

The game was over for West Virginia in the first five minutes. Harris hurt himself on the third play of the game. "I can't move my right arm," he reported to his coach. Nehlen had little time to fret over his quarterback when the safety broke his leg. Two other players joined the injured list, and West Virginia fell to Notre Dame 34–21.

I wonder what would have happened if luck hadn't turned on West Virginia.

Still, Nehlen had the opportunity to get lucky in other ways. The job offers at the end of the 1988 season came pouring in. Merry Ann Nehlen couldn't see the point of cashing in those chips. She thought they had already "hit the jackpot." So they didn't cash in, and Nehlen stayed put.

"How many cars can we drive?" she wanted to know. "How many houses can we have? Our kids are here…what's the big deal? We're not bright lights people."

And though it took a few years, the luck reoccurred, as many dreams do. In 1993, Nehlen took in another stray, quarterback Jake Kelchner, who had left Notre Dame. Although he was, like so many of West Virginia's greats, from Pennsylvania, he was no Jeff Hostetler, that former Penn State transfer, that future son-in-law. Instead, Kelchner came to Nehlen under a cloud. He was expelled from Notre Dame after being arrested for driving while intoxicated, pleading guilty to reckless driving. Nehlen, though, was able to use him to full advantage. By the middle of the 1993 season, Kelchner led the country in pass efficiency.

That their schedule consisted, in part, of Eastern Michigan, Maryland, Missouri, Pitt, Rutgers, and Temple—with a combined record of 17–47–1—wasn't likely to impress the press.

Unfortunately, that they engaged in perennial confrontations against teams like Syracuse, which were charged with intense emotion, failed to impress as well.

The emotion for the 1993 Syracuse game had been sustained through many seasons, but had been especially charged in 1992, when a brawl brought on by questionable penalties fostered a 20–17 Syracuse victory. In 1993, the West Virginia players sought revenge, and found it to be sweet, shutting Syracuse out through three and a half quarters. Then, with 4:45 left in the game, ESPN, strangely, switched coverage to the UCLA–Arizona game. Fans were not able to see the final conclusive touchdown that set West Virginia's victory at 43–0.

To the press, a conclusive West Virginia win scarcely mattered.

And then West Virginia came up against Miami. But even that victory was skewed by the press.

According to them, the game was simply a litany of Miami mistakes. Quarterback Ryan Collins fumbled a snap on Miami's first possession; later in the first half, he let a snap bounce off his stomach and tumble to the ground. Collins also threw two interceptions, and tailback James Stewart fumbled as well.

Anyone who knows football knows mistakes don't happen in a vacuum; most frequently, a team cornered by a superior opponent makes them. But the press had soured on West Virginia and on Nehlen. Despite an undefeated season, once-beaten Florida State and Notre Dame both remained in front of them in the AP poll, and Florida State received the bid to play number one Nebraska in the Orange Bowl for the national championship, while West Virginia earned only a Sugar Bowl berth versus eighth-ranked Florida.

When Nehlen vocalized frustration, he earned vitriol from reporters. *Sports Illustrated* writer Austin Murphy opened an article by stating that Nehlen's "belly aching" had "reached a crescendo." Murphy also responded to Nehlen's claim that excluding West Virginia from the title game would be "the biggest misjustice in the world" with venomous sarcasm: "Way to keep things in perspective, coach."

A dream so tainted by harsh colorings could only end in nightmare. The *Charleston Gazette*'s headline, "Dream Season Ends in Nightmarish Defeat," captured the layers of disappointment implicit in Nehlen's 41–7 Sugar Bowl loss to Florida. Not only did the game tarnish an undefeated record and any chance at a share in the national championship; it gave the press an opportunity to say, "I told you so."

From then on, the press held the better hand.

In 1996, a syndicated columnist bestowed on Nehlen the "Blockhead of the Season Award" after back-to-back Big East losses, first to Miami, then to Syracuse. In both games, West Virginia's opponent capitalized on blocked punts, Miami returning one for a touchdown with twenty-nine seconds remaining in the game to secure a 10–7 victory. After the loss to Syracuse, Nehlen commented to the press, "It's crazy. I've never had so much trouble with a blocked punt." Reporter Lenn Robbins retorted, "But it's not crazy. Just poor coaching."

Why does defeat obliterate the memory of great success? Why does defeat invite cruelty?

This past year, one shy of his two hundredth victory, Nehlen's team fell first to Virginia Tech 48–20 and then to Syracuse 31–27.

Also this past year, Nehlen chose to retire at sixty five, right on the money, as if he were retiring from anything— management, civil service, education—about which he had long ceased to care. He had told me that "If I didn't think I was doin' a good job, I'm outta here."

When he first informed me of his stance, I took it to mean he would never leave. After he announced his retirement, I listened again to my interview tapes. He sounded like Priam after Hector died.

When, after the 2000 Syracuse game, he spoke to the press, he endeavored to sound chipper. He said, "I want to check around and see if there's anything else to do." His words, to me, rang false.

At the same time, Dick Tomey—whose first coaching days were as a graduate assistant at Miami in 1962 and 1963 under Nehlen's former hero John Pont and former coach Bo Schembechler—left Arizona. Also, Larry Smith—a fellow Bowling Green graduate—left Missouri. Both Tomey and Smith had, in the past few years, accumulated more losses than the prestige of a big-name university could allow. Smith's contract had been under scrutiny the entire season, so his retirement grew more sadly inevitable with every loss his team suffered.

Thinking of men like Nehlen, Tomey, and Smith, I asked Sid Gillman, "What makes a great coach?"

"Winning," he quickly quipped.

When I queried other coaches on this topic, they all, like Bo Schembechler, spoke of teaching, of shaping their players into men. In light of their thoughtfulness, Gillman's response seemed horribly cynical.

But I think now that the other coaches were just too timid to tell the truth. Losing had hurt or frightened them so badly, they did not want to articulate how much they had wanted, how much time and energy they had expended, how much of their personal and family life they had neglected, to win.

Don Nehlen's last home game was a resounding victory over East Carolina. At the end of the game, Merry Ann Nehlen hung over a railing cloaked in a fur coat with tears in her eyes. He had won enough to earn her the coat, but not to continue beyond that game.

Now, just as Bill Mallory continues on in Bloomington, the site of his triumph and fall, Nehlen has no intention of leaving Morgantown, West Virginia. It's where his children and his memories live on.

Afterword:
My Dad

Once, my father watched me run. When I was a sophomore
in high school I was the swiftest girl on my track team in the
four hundred meters. In the world at large that status was
tested in the first meet of the season, against a team perenni-
ally better than ours. As I huddled among fellow runners,
watching other events while I waited for a reasonable time to
begin my warm-ups, one of my friends said, "Look at that guy
on the bleachers." Because girls' track, at least where I went
to school, attracted few, if any, spectators, we all turned to see
the spectacle. Alone in the sagging center row of bleachers
sat my father, windbreaker on, hands in his pockets. I turned
away immediately, peeled my sweats, and began to stretch.
After my race, which I won by a little over a second—thank
God—I walked down the path to the gymnasium, into the
locker room, thrust my head over a toilet, and threw up. Just in

time, I made it back to the track to line up for the eight hundred meters.

Looking back, my reaction to the presence of my father seems extreme but understandable. I had learned only to watch, not to be watched.

When I say I learned to watch, I do not mean that I became an expert on football at an early age. In fact, for years the games were tedious blurs, punctured periodically by the clear image of a touchdown. No one ever explained the game to me; I grew to understand it through osmosis and desperation. To this day, I am unable to recognize a holding penalty.

When I say I learned to watch I mean that I came to define myself as a person who watches others. The greatest joy was and still is watching those I love do what they do.

Always, my father was first and best. Because he gave me plenty to watch, he gave me plenty of joy.

Being his daughter wasn't always easy. Though football colored every season, fall was overwhelming. Tension mounted when, on Friday night, my father placed the program for the next day's game onto the counter. The glossy cover confirmed that the game was unavoidable.

Then, on Saturday morning, just around dawn, my father would embark on his weekly ritual of vacuuming the house. In the seventies, he made do with an upright Hoover, but by the early eighties, he had two high-tech machines that my brother dubbed "R2D2" and "C3PO." As soon as the whir of the vacuum pierced the pinkish air, my brother and sisters and I would cramp up in our beds, more scared than cats. Then we settled into our pillows, knowing sleep time was over. We wouldn't dream of asking our father to stop . . . not on Saturday morning before the game.

Even in the off-season, little things could make him boil. Luckily, we knew when he was most susceptible: football Saturdays and Christmas.

Primarily, he hated to put up the tree. So when he was out recruiting, when he drove through Ohio and Indiana and Michigan and Kentucky, trying to talk to kids who suspected that the Ivy League was a family of poisonous plants, my mother and sisters and I bought a tree, shoved it through the front door, stood it in the living room, decorated it, and vacuumed up the fallen needles.

Because my father bears some resemblance to Woody Hayes—the bulky head, the clumsy voice, the uncomfortable way he wears clothes, the seasonal disregard for all things unrelated to football—his irrational hostility toward Christmas trees makes me wonder about all football coaches. At no time are they ever really able to leave the pressures of winning behind.

But even when Yale was losing in the eighties, I made it to games. Once, to get to Penn for a late October game, I borrowed a friend's car and stripped the gears because I didn't know how to drive stick. I sold my complete works of

Shakespeare and several Norton Anthologies to buy a plane ticket home for the Yale-Harvard game. When Yale won, my world smiled. When Yale lost, I cried.

When my father announced his retirement at the close of the 1993 season, I was beside myself. I wasn't there for his last game. There is still an emptiness: a lined field with no players, no sounds, no emotions.

No man for flashy banquets, my father invited to brunch at our house one of his last groups of senior running backs— Chris Kouri, Jim Gouveia, and Maurice Saah—as well as two players from Ohio—Matt Garretson and Eric Kaup. They were scheduled to arrive with their families at noon on Sunday of graduation weekend.

At nine or so that Sunday morning, my sisters Mary and Cathy and I went into the kitchen. The light through the windows was warming the room. There was no coffee in the pot, no newspaper on the table; my parents were nowhere to be seen. They had, apparently, gone to church.

We made quiches and salads and an enormous batch of chocolate chip cookies. We sped (sorry Dad) to the store to buy juice and napkins. When we got back, the phone rang: the families were all coming an hour early.

Just then, my parents returned from church.

All morning, my father's champagne glass never emptied. He wandered past conversations, smiling, till he took his familiar seat at the kitchen table. As if they heard a silent call, his players emerged from different corners of the house and gathered around him.

He looked from one to the other. "You were the best team I ever coached."

The hyperbole seemed excessive, even from my father. I began to protest, but I saw the expression on the players' faces. They were in a football heaven where they floated, as if in a Thanksgiving parade, along with Calvin Hill, Brian Dowling, Dick Jauron, Pudge Heffelfinger, even Walter Camp. To burst those balloons would destroy whole lives.

Besides, they were in my house because they loved my father too much for hyperbole.

They're not the only ones who felt that way. On my way to interview Woody Hayes's son Steve in Columbus, I visited with another of my father's former players, Jeff Kaplan. In the office from which he runs a premier treatment center for critically ill children, we chatted about my father.

"Woody was a great man," said Kaplan. "But your father... he changed people's lives."

That's the funny thing about my Dad. He wears plaid pants with striped shirts. His ears sprout thick brushes of hair. As soon as he touches a remote control, he screws up all the commands. Until a year or two ago, he rented the two rotary telephones in our home, paying thousands for a service that had long since become obsolete. Every steak he ever had was the "best" steak he ever had. When he's washing dishes, he calls my mother's name out loud. He is at the same time so simple and so powerful.

How did he change me? It's hard to say. When Shemy Schembechler responded to that question by glibly listing a series of lessons he learned from Bo, I was at first envious, then unconvinced. It seemed to me that Shemy settled for easy answers because he knows his father changed him, but he's not sure how.

What do our fathers teach us? Not clichés, not generalities, not abstractions. Values like discipline, commitment, and passion cannot be isolated into lessons. They're inseparable from the man, the life; they are so tangled up with grumpiness, self-absorption, violence, and fear that all qualities appear the same. They teach us, as best they can, how to live.

While I was growing up, one of the most common sights in my house was my father sitting at the kitchen table. Generally, he drifted there in the late afternoon, made up a plate of sliced cheddar and damp saltines, poured a glass of wine full to the lip, and settled down at the old wooden table with a small pad of paper and a pencil in front of him. While my mother prepared dinner, my father tattooed sheet after sheet with clusters of *X*s and *O*s...and I do not mean hugs and kisses. It was another love. He was writing football narratives; some he had studied, some observed, some applied, some invented on the spot. As fast as the pads piled up, my mother cleared them out, but I could always find one or two hiding beneath junk mail. If I were to line up the pages he filled in his nearly three decades at Yale, the line would stretch from New Haven to South Bend, then back again with a few detours through Ann Arbor, Bloomington, and several dozen towns along the Ohio River.

For years I regarded my father's scribblings as a behavior akin to Uncle Billy tying strings around his finger to remember things. A lovable eccentricity, neither harmful nor useful. Tic-tac-toe, though the visual and intellectual equivalent of his doodles, would at least be more sociable. "What are you doing, Dad... drawing *X*s and *O*s?" I giggled as I snuck bits of cheese.

But, now I know, that was the language he spoke—as did Sid Gillman and every other Ohio coach before him—when he was performing the drama of football for the world to watch.

Now, no one watches my father. At dawn, or even earlier, in the wintertime, my father walks our dog, Lucy, talking to her more than he ever talked to any of his daughters. That's okay. Lucy actually looks a lot like me—black hair, lean legs—so I like to think he confides in Lucy all the things he's already said to me in other, better ways.

Chronology

1946   Sid Gillman adapts his own version of the T formation when coaching Paul Dietzel and Ara Parseghian at Miami of Ohio.

1949   After a brief stint at Army under Red Blaik, Sid Gillman goes to Cincinnati where he begins to accumulate a record of 50–13–1.

For Paul Dietzel the long apprenticeship begins as assistant coach to the greats: Sid Gillman, Bear Bryant, Red Blaik.

Woody Hayes moves from Denison to coach at Miami; inherits a team containing John Pont, Bo Schembechler, and Carm Cozza.

1950   John Pont has a stellar season as running back for the season culminating in a Miami victory over Cincinnati in the Snow Bowl game; Pont's number 42 later becomes the first of only two jerseys retired by Miami.

1951   Woody Hayes is chosen for the coveted Ohio State coaching job over the Ohio legend Paul Brown.

Ara Parseghian is named head coach at Miami despite criticism from Paul Brown: "Ara doesn't know what he doesn't know."

1952   Paul Dietzel, as assistant coach under Bear Bryant, stands up to Bryant's totalitarian style.

When Miami plays Wichita State, Ara Parseghian makes a statement against racism by fighting the hotel that tried to turn away African American player Boxcar Bailey.

Bo Schembechler becomes assistant to Woody Hayes, a job he keeps until 1962, thus furthering a relationship that defines his career.

1954   Woody Hayes rectifies a rocky start at Ohio State by beating Michigan in the rain: 21–7.

Bill Mallory begins playing at Miami for Ara Parseghian. He later continues his career under John Pont.

1955   Paul Dietzel, assistant at Army, earns the head coaching position at LSU through Army connection Biff Jones.

1956   John Pont takes over as Miami head coach when Parseghian moves on to Northwestern University.

1958   Paul Dietzel puts together the third-string wonders: the "Chinese Bandits"; Dietzel is named Coach of the Year.

Ara Parseghian turns Northwestern from an 0–9 season to second in Big Ten, beating Michigan and Ohio State.

1959   Nick Mourouzis as quarterback leads Miami in an outstanding game against Bowling Green, making Mourouzis a favorite of John Pont.

LSU's Billy Cannon wins the Heisman Trophy.

1960   Sid Gillman invents the "moving pocket" with the L.A. Chargers.

1962   John Pont coaches Miami to an upset of Purdue, attracting the attention of Chicago-area Yale alum who spark interest in Pont as potential Yale coach.

1963   Sid Gillman coaches the San Diego Chargers to the AFL championship; they are proclaimed the best team in the country by Chicago Bears' coach George Halas.

John Pont begins his first season at Yale University with Carm Cozza as one of his assistant coaches.

1964   Ara Parseghian leaves Northwestern to take over as head coach for a losing Notre Dame program; he immediately shifts all the personnel on the team to new positions.

1966   Paul Dietzel takes on a new kind of role as head coach and athletic director at the University of South Carolina: raising funds for a program that was struggling financially.

Ara Parseghian coaches Notre Dame to a 10–10 tie with Michigan State; the strategy calls Parseghian's coaching into question, despite the fact that Notre Dame won the national championship.

1968   John Pont coaches his Indiana team to the first Rose Bowl in Indiana history.

Carm Cozza coaches Yale to a 28–28 tie with Harvard despite the presence of such greats on the team as Brian Dowling and Calvin Hill.

Nick Mourouzis is in a car accident while driving with John Pont on a recruiting trip in Ohio.

1969   Bo Schembechler beats number one–ranked Ohio State in Ann Arbor, earning his team a Rose Bowl berth; he suffers a heart attack just before the Rose Bowl game.

Bill Mallory moves from his position as assistant coach at Ohio State to assume the head coach position at Miami.

1970   Woody Hayes encourages his Ohio State team to rebound from the previous year's loss to beat Michigan with the line: "This one literally is for a lifetime." His team goes on to defeat USC in the Rose Bowl.

Carm Cozza begins a decade in which his teams win or share four Ivy League titles and come in second four times.

A trial of Black Panther leaders held in New Haven shuts down Yale University, reflecting the political conflicts that underscored life for the football team.

1974   Woody Hayes's star Archie Griffin earns the first of his two Heisman Trophys.

Sid Gillman wins Coach of the Year at the helm of the Houston Oilers.

1975   Ara Parseghian retires from his position as head coach at Notre Dame after Orange Bowl defeat of Bear Bryant's Alabama, leaving football to spend more time with his family.

1977   John Pont retires from his position as head coach at Northwestern.

1978   On national television, while Ohio State is losing to Clemson in the Gator Bowl, Woody Hayes punches a Clemson player.

1979   Sid Gillman joins Dick Vermeil's staff at the Philadelphia Eagles. His expertise helps them get to the Super Bowl in 1980.

1980   Bo Schembechler earns his first Rose Bowl win, over Washington, breaking a ten-year jinx.

Bill Mallory, who left the University of Colorado for reasons of moral difference, goes to Northern Illinois.

Don Nehlen becomes head coach at West Virginia.

1981   Nick Mourouzis becomes head coach at DePauw University.

1982   Mallory's son, Mike Mallory, heads to Michigan to play for Bo Schembechler; over the years, two of Mike's younger brothers follow him to Ann Arbor.

In West Virginia's season opener against Oklahoma, West Virginia wins, establishing quarterback Jeff Hostetler as a force to be reckoned with.

1983   Bill Mallory takes his Northern Illinois team to the California Bowl.

1984   Bill Mallory follows in his old coach John Pont's shoes by taking the head coaching job at Indiana.

1989   Don Nehlen's West Virginia team, after a perfect season, finds itself in contention for the national championship, but loses to Notre Dame in the Fiesta Bowl.

1990   John Pont returns to college coaching by launching a brand new program at Mount St. Joseph, formerly an all-women's college.

1996   Indiana athletic director Clarence Doninger announces his intent to fire head coach Bill Mallory.

1999   A plane over West Virginia's Mountaineer Stadium proclaims, NEHLEN MUST GO.

Memorable Games
of the Golden Age

1950 Cincinnati vs. Miami of Ohio—In the game that became known as "The Snow Bowl," Woody Hayes led the Miami team to a 28–0 victory through an unexpected blizzard.

1950 Michigan vs. Ohio State—On the same day as the Snow Bowl, Michigan defeated Ohio State by a score of 9–3.

1955 Miami of Ohio vs. Bowling Green—Coached by Ara Parseghian, Miami scored a 7–0 victory over a Bowling Green team led by quarterback Don Nehlen.

1958 LSU vs. Alabama—During Bear Bryant's first year at Alabama, Paul Dietzel led LSU to a 13–3 victory.

1958 Miami of Ohio vs. Bowling Green—John Pont coached the Miami team to a victory of 28–14.

1959 LSU vs. Ole Miss—Paul Dietzel led the LSU team to a 7–6 win over arch rival Ole Miss.

1963 Army vs. Navy—With Paul Dietzel at the head of Army's team, Army was defeated by Navy 21–15.

1966 Notre Dame vs. Michigan State—Notre Dame, led by Ara Parseghian, tied Michigan State 10–10.

1967   Indiana vs. Minnesota—Minnesota dominated John Pont's Indiana team in a 33–7 victory, Indiana's only loss of the regular season.

1968   Harvard vs. Yale—A score of 29–29 forced Yale and Harvard to share the Ivy League crown.

1969   Ohio State vs. Michigan—Bo Schembechler led the Michigan team to victory in a 24–12 win over Woody Hayes's team.

1972   Yale vs. Harvard—Dick Jauron led Yale to a 28–17 victory over Harvard in Cambridge, where Yale had not won in twelve years.

1973   Sugar Bowl: Notre Dame vs. Alabama—Notre Dame, led by Parseghian, defeated Alabama, 24–23.

1973   Michigan vs. Ohio State—Big Ten commissioners sent Ohio State to the Rose Bowl to represent the conference against USC after a 10–10 tie.

1974   Rose Bowl: Ohio State vs. USC—Ohio State was victorious in a 42–21 game.

1975   Princeton vs. Yale—Princeton was defeated, 6–0, with the help of Gary Fencik.

1978   Gator Bowl: Clemson vs. Ohio State—A punch thrown at a Clemson player marked the end of Woody Hayes's career.

1982   West Virginia vs. Oklahoma—In Jeff Hostetler's WVU debut, Don Nehlen's West Virginia squad scored a 41–27 win over Oklahoma.

1987   Indiana vs. Ohio State—Bill Mallory led an Indiana win of 31–10.

1988   West Virginia vs. Penn State—West Virginia, led by Don Nehlen, posted a 51–30 upset over Penn State.

1989   Rose Bowl: USC vs. Michigan—Bo Schembechler led Michigan to victory, 22–14.

About the Coaches

Sid Gillman was born in Minneapolis, Minnesota, the son of a movie theater owner. While head coach at Miami of Ohio from 1944 to 1947, among the players he worked with and inspired were Ara Parseghian and Paul Dietzel. After tremendous success at the University of Cincinnati (with a record of 50–13–1), he moved on to professional football, first the L.A. Rams, then the L.A. Chargers, which became the San Diego Chargers. He is credited by other strategic innovators such as San Francisco's Bill Walsh with fathering the "West Coast Offense." He is the only coach inducted into both the college and professional football halls of fame. He currently lives in La Costa, California.

Woody Hayes, from Newcomerstown, Ohio, played football and studied history at Denison University. During his brief time as head coach at Miami of Ohio (1949–1950), he experienced so much success—as a result, in part, of such athletes as John Pont, Carm Cozza, and Bo Schembechler—that he secured the coveted Ohio State position, which he kept for twenty-eight years. He was named National Coach of the Year in 1957; his teams earned three national championships and thirteen Big Ten titles; and he coached the only player—Archie Griffin—to receive the Heisman Trophy twice. Woody Hayes's son Steve currently lives in Columbus, Ohio.

Ara Parseghian was born in Akron, Ohio, and was a three-season athlete at Miami of Ohio. After serving as Miami's head coach from 1951 to 1955, he went on to resurrect the struggling programs first at Northwestern, then at Notre Dame. His first year at Notre Dame (1964) earned him a near-perfect season and a Heisman Trophy winner in quarterback John Huarte. He earned the honor of National Coach of the Year that same year. He remained at Notre Dame until 1974. He currently acts as a fund-raiser for research on Niemann-Pick type C disease. He lives in South Bend, Indiana.

John Pont, born in Canton, Ohio, played football for Woody Hayes and Ara Parseghian at Miami of Ohio. His number 42 jersey was the first ever to be retired by a Miami athletic team. He coached at Miami, at Yale, and then at Indiana. There, he was the first coach to take the Hoosiers to the Rose Bowl. He was named National Coach of the Year in 1967. After coaching at Northwestern, he took a break from football; then he returned to start a football program at a formerly all-women's college: Mount St. Joseph. He is currently coaching in Japan. He divides his time between Tokyo and Oxford, Ohio.

Paul Dietzel hails from Mansfield, Ohio. In high school, his football team yearly played and once defeated Paul Brown's famous Massillon team. After a stint in the Air Force, he began studies at Miami of Ohio, where he was coached by Sid Gillman, who would become a father figure to him. He acted as an assistant to Gillman at Cincinnati, to Red Blaik at Army, and to Bear Bryant at Kentucky. As head coach at LSU, Dietzel invented a system of substitution that included the famous third-string team: the Chinese Bandits. The bandits helped earn him the National Championship and National Coach of the Year honors in 1958. He went on to coach at Army and South Carolina. He now lives in Beech Mountain, North Carolina.

Bo Schembechler is from Barberton, Ohio. After playing at Miami, he acted as an assistant to the great Doyt Perry at Bowling Green, to Ara Parseghian at Northwestern, and to Woody Hayes at Ohio State; then he returned to Miami as head coach. His relationship with Hayes, first coached by him, then assistant to him, then rivals with him, spawned decades of great football. In Schembechler's first season as head coach on the University of Michigan's team, 1969, he defeated Hayes's number one–ranked program, earning him a trip to the Rose Bowl and National Coach of the Year honors. He remained with Michigan's program until 1989. He is currently living in Ann Arbor, Michigan.

Carm Cozza was born in Parma, Ohio, just outside Cleveland, and was, as a boy, a fan of the Cleveland Indians. He played quarterback for Miami of

Ohio, and was later assistant at Miami to John Pont. He moved with Pont to Yale University, where he stayed on as head coach after Pont's departure in 1964. He remained there for thirty-two years, earning Yale ten Ivy League championships. He currently lives in New Haven, Connecticut.

Bill Mallory, from Sandusky, Ohio, has a family tradition in football. His father coached high school ball; he and his brothers played at Miami of Ohio; his three sons played at Michigan under Bo Schembechler and are all three currently football coaches. He was brought to Miami by Ara Parseghian, and was coached by Parseghian and John Pont. He served as an assistant coach under Woody Hayes at Ohio State, Carm Cozza at Yale, and Doyt Perry at Bowling Green. Mallory's head coaching career took him from Miami, to Colorado, to Northern Illinois, and finally to Indiana, where he remained from 1984 to 1996. He currently lives in Bloomington, Indiana.

Don Nehlen, a native of Canton, Ohio, played football at Bowling Green, coached by Doyt Perry. As starting quarterback, Nehlen's record there was 21–2–4. At the urging of Perry, who moved on to the role of Bowling Green athletic director, Nehlen became head coach of the program at his alma mater. After eight seasons there, he moved on to an assistant's position at Michigan, working under Bo Schembechler. In 1980, he began his twenty-year career at West Virginia. At the time of his retirement in 2000, he had earned over two hundred career victories. He currently lives in Morgantown, West Virginia.

Nick Mourouzis, a native of Uhrichsville, Ohio, was John Pont's star quarterback at Miami of Ohio. Mourouzis joined Pont's staff as an assistant during Pont's tenure at Indiana, and stayed with him through the difficult years at Northwestern. When Pont went into retirement from football, Mourouzis took the position as head coach of DePauw University's team. He remains at DePauw today.

Index